Fair Sunshine

Fair Sunshine

Character studies of the Scottish Covenanters

JOCK PURVES

The Banner of Truth Trust *78b Chiltern Street London* W1

The material in this volume consists of two works
Sweet Believing 1948 and *Fair Sunshine* 1957
This revised edition published under the title *Fair Sunshine* by
The Banner of Truth Trust 1968

Set in 11 on 13 pt Monotype Fournier
and printed in Great Britain by
Hazell Watson & Viney Ltd Aylesbury Bucks

Preface

A friend once asked me to write a few papers on the Scottish Coven-anters for his evangelical magazine and I complied with his request. Sometime later he suggested that I should gather them together and make a book of them. I gathered them together and looked at them but they were far from enough for that purpose. They were again put away, but happening to look at them one day hope sprang up that they might be the foundation of a book. The outcome of further work on them was the two books Sweet Believing *and* Fair Sunshine, *both published by the Stirling Tract Enterprise.*

The Banner of Truth Trust has now brought the two works together in one volume. The order of the character studies in the original volumes has been retained but the whole has undergone a thorough revision. In the place of the texts of the National Covenant and the Solemn League and Covenant there is included an interesting 'Outline of Scottish "Covenant History" in the 17th Century', compiled by Mr S. M. Houghton. It is a useful guide to readers who could learn more about a people and their Covenants with God in Christ.

I am glad of this reprint, for the witness of the Covenanters will ever be an example for Christians. Simply yet clearly they had in-scribed upon some of their banners what they believed and that for which they nobly lived and died: 'For the Word of God and the Testimony of Jesus'; 'For Christ's Crown and Covenant'. There is a high and holy confession of faith in these words. And they are certainly apt for our own day.

JOCK PURVES

Farewell, beloved sufferers, and followers of the Lamb . . .
Farewell, night wanderings, cold and weariness for Christ . . .
Farewell, holy Scriptures wherewith my soul has been many a
day refreshed . . . *Farewell, reading, singing and praying* . . .
Farewell, sweet believing. Welcome, immediate presence of
God and His Son Jesus Christ, who only has redeemed me
with His blood.

Covenanters under sentence of death

What shall I say in this great day of the Lord, wherein in
the midst of a cloud, I have found a fair sunshine. I can
wish no more for you, but that the Lord may comfort you, and
shine upon you as He does upon me, and give you that same
sense of His love in staying in the world, as I have in going
out of it.

Letter of Archibald Campbell, ninth earl of Argyle, Covenanter, to
his daughter-in-law, Lady Sophia Lindsay, written on the day of his
execution in Edinburgh.

Contents

Chronological Summary

1560 Reformed Faith established as national religion of Scotland.

1580 Protestant leaders pledge themselves to support the Reformed doctrine and discipline in *The National Covenant*.

1603 Union of the Crowns [James VI of Scotland becomes James I of England].

1610 Bishops established in Scotland by royal authority.

1618 The Five Articles of Perth. The King seeks to conform Scottish worship to the pattern of the Anglican Church.

1625 Accession of Charles I who pursues his father's policy.

1637 Rejection of Archbishop Laud's Liturgy. Jenny Geddes throws stool in St Giles.

1638 Signing of the National Covenant. Presbyterianism re-established and the independence of the Church re-asserted.

1639-40 First and Second Bishops' Wars.

1642-48 First and Second Civil Wars.

1643 Signing of the Solemn League and Covenant. English Puritans and Scottish Presbyterians pledge their nations to uniformity in religion according to the Word of God.

1643-49 Westminster Assembly of Divines.

1651 The Scots crown Charles II at Scone but Oliver Cromwell subdues their country.

1660 The Restoration of the monarchy. Charles II throws off his former allegiance to the Scottish Presbyterians.

1661 Prelacy re-established by law.

Chronological Summary

1662 Over three hundred ministers turned out of their parishes. Field-preaching and Conventicles introduced.

1663 Government attempts to limit Conventicles. Persecution commences.

1666 Covenanter rising ends with defeat at Rullion Green.

1669 A Declaration of Indulgence which results in division of Covenanters into the 'indulged' and the 'non-indulged'.

1670 'Field-meetings' made treasonable and preaching at such meetings becomes a capital offence.

1679 Murder of Archbishop Sharp [3 May].
Covenanters defeat Government forces at Drumclog [1 June]
Covenanters defeated at Bothwell Bridge [22 June]

1680 Covenanters defeated at Ayrsmoss. Richard Cameron killed.

1684-85 'The Killing Times' – the period of hottest persecution.

1685 Accession of James II.

1688 Capture and execution of James Renwick, the last of the Covenanting martyrs.
The Glorious Revolution. The Church of Scotland is restored to her spiritual freedom.

James Guthrie

James Guthrie

They have set his head on the Netherbow,
  To scorch in the summer air;
And months go by, and the winter's snow
  Falls white on its thin grey hair.
And still that same look that in death he wore
  Is sealed on the solemn brow —
A look as of one who had travailed sore,
  But whose pangs were ended now.

HARRIET STUART MENTEITH, Lays of the Kirk and Covenant

Some of our Zaccheus-like men, as full of faith and as unerring in aim as David, have, like him, been slayers of giants. James Guthrie was one of them. He and Cromwell knew each other, and the mighty Puritan referred to him as 'the short little man who could not bow.' Covenanter and Puritan! Shall we ever see their like again? What a glorious heritage they have left to us, though somewhat now 'the wild boar from the wood doth waste it.'

As Joses, by the generosity of his character, won the name of Barnabas, Son of Consolation, so James Guthrie, by the stability of his character, earned the name of Sickerfoot [Sure of Foot]. And such indeed was he until he mounted the ladder to the scaffold, where he spoke for an hour, surefooted on the Rock, dying firm in his Covenanting principles. In life and death, he fulfilled the Scripture, 'steadfast, unmovable, always abounding in the work of the Lord.'

One day a friend would have had him compromise a little. Said he, 'Mr Guthrie, we have an old Scots proverb, "Jouk [duck] that the wave may gang oure ye! Will ye nae jouk a wee bit?"' And gravely Guthrie replied, 'There is nae jouking in the Cause of Christ!' And so it was. That unbending, sure-footed, non-ducking soldier of God held his head high until it was taken from him, and shamefully set aloft upon a pike above the thronging Netherbow Port of Edinburgh. There it bleached for twenty-seven years, till lover of the free Gospel Sandie Hamilton, a student for the Covenanting ministry, climbed the sombre Port at the risk of his life, and taking down the skull, buried it reverently away.

James Guthrie had much whereof he might have trusted in the flesh, amongst which was a very liberal education, given not with the object of making him a Covenanting minister. But, meeting with 'yours in his sweet Lord Jesus, Samuel Rutherford,' all he had learned against the non-conforming Presbyterians vanished forever, and among them he became a preacher of the Gospel in 1638, the year when the National Covenant was signed. His name, too, is set there on that great spiritual Magna Charta. While on his way to pen his name, he met the hangman. This moved him somewhat, and, feeling that it was prophetic, it made him walk up and down a little before he went forward. But his signature is there in martyr lustre with the honoured names of those thousands of others on that great parchment of deerskin, 'the holiest thing in all Scotland, a vow registered in Heaven.' Two months before he died, he boldly confessed to the Parliament, 'I am not ashamed to give God the glory that until 1638 I was treading other steps.'

The last twelve years of his life were spent in Stirling, the grey fortress town whose castled rock is ever a symbol of him. Here he lived and devotedly wrought for Christ and His Kirk. Steady in temper, he believed in the loosening up of the knots of any argument before engaging in further reasoning. Fervent in spirit, and not slothful in business, he was careful, loving and true. An undaunted fighter in a worthwhile cause, and a hater of everything lower than true godliness, such as he was soon, and always, in conflict with the loose-living King Charles Stuart and his like Committees. He utterly refused such a profane ruler any authority in the affairs of the Church. Although dismissed after one big trial, his refusal to allow the king any power over the conscience of a Christian was made much of against him in his last trials, ten years later.

He helped to write the searching pamphlet, *The Causes of the Lord's Wrath against Scotland*, and this paper was the principal pretext for his condemnation and execution. It had the honour of being put on a par with *Lex Rex* by Samuel Rutherford, and copies of both books were publicly burned by the common hangman. To hold a copy of either work was treason against King and government. The purpose of these writings was said to be 'to corrupt the minds of his majesty's loyal subjects, to alienate and withdraw them from that duty of love and obedience that they owe unto his sacred person and greatness, stirring them up against his majesty and kingly government, and containing many things injurious to the king's majesty's person and authority.' But, above all that base slander, the principles they taught are those upon which the true British Constitution is based. It was a noxious doctrine that Erastus taught when he averred that a king was sovereign and supreme in all matters temporal and spiritual, and that if a Church exercised powers of government and discipline in her own lawful sphere, it broke in on the authority of the magistrate. Every page of the proscribed books is for the Crown Rights of the Redeemer in His Church, the freedom of the conscience, and against the so-called Divine Right of Kings.

The wordy indictment set forth against James Guthrie gives some vivid idea of his amazing activity. 'He did contrive, complot, counsel, consult, draw up, frame, invent, spread abroad or disperse – speak, preach, declaim or utter – divers and sundry vile seditions and treasonable remonstrances, declarations, petitions, instructions, letters, speeches, preachings, declamations and other expressions tending to the vilifying and contemning, slander and reproach of His Majesty, his progenitors, his person, majesty, dignity, authority, prerogative royal, and government.'

Shortly after the Restoration of Charles II, in 1660, Guthrie, with others, was apprehended and cast into prison. In February of 1661, he was tried, and in April of that year he made a defence before the well-named Drunken Parliament. It concludes with these words, 'My Lord, my conscience I cannot submit. But this old crazy body and mortal flesh I do submit, to do with it whatsoever ye will, whether by death, or banishment, or imprisonment, or anything else; only I beseech you to ponder well what profit there is in my blood. It is not the extinguishing of me or of many others that will extinguish the Covenant or work of the Reformation since 1638. My blood, bondage or banishment will contribute more for the propagation of these things than my life in liberty would do, though I should live many years.' At the close of this speech, some members withdrew, saying that they would have no part in his death, and one made a strong appeal urging banishment. But his judges were baying for his blood, and he, with Captain William Govan, a fit companion, was sentenced to be hanged at Edinburgh Cross on 1 June 1661. The head of Guthrie was to be stuck on a pike high above the Netherbow Port, his estate confiscated, and his family arms torn. The head of Govan, pike-stuck, was likewise to be high up on the West Port. On receiving this sentence, Guthrie said to the members of the Drunken Parliament, 'My Lords, let never this sentence affect you more than it does me, and let never my blood be required from the King's family.' But it was required, with the blood of many others, in the fullness of time.

While lying in the Tolbooth, he saw Archibald Campbell, Marquis of Argyle, 'not afraid,' as Argyle said, 'to be surprised by fear,' going forth with Christian dignity to his martyrdom. Said Guthrie, 'Such is my respect for your Lordship that were I not under sentence of death myself I could cheerfully die for your Lordship.' There was but a week between their meeting and their parting. He told his wife, 'I am more fortunate than the Great Marquis, for my Lord was beheaded, but I am to be hanged on a tree as my Saviour was.' His wife wept sorely when for the last time she parted from him. 'I do but trouble you,' she said. 'I must now part from you.' And he replied, 'Henceforth I know no man after the flesh.'

James Cowie, his dear friend and manservant, was with him in the Tolbooth, and he tells us that James Guthrie ever kept through his busy life his own personal fellowship with Christ, in the fresh joyous bloom of his new birth, as if he had been but a young convert; and thus it wondrously was till his last day on earth dawned, and the summer sun streamed in through the iron bars of his cell windows. Sure-of-Foot arose at about four o'clock for worship, and was asked by Cowie how he was. 'Very well,' said Guthrie. 'This is the day that the Lord hath made; let us rejoice and be glad in it.' Soon was to be fulfilled the prophecy of his godly cousin, William Guthrie, of

James Guthrie

Fenwick, author of the spiritual classic, *The Christian's Great Interest*. He had said, 'Ye will have the advantage of me, James, for ye will die honourably before many witnesses with a rope about your neck, and I shall die whinging upon a wee pickle straw.'[1] This was the day and the Lord had made it, and his confessed desire – called by him a lust – that he should die for his Saviour, was to be granted.

His two little children, Sophia and William, came to see him. Taking five-year-old William on his knee, he said to him, 'Willie, the day will come when they will cast up to you that your father was hanged. But be not thou ashamed, lad. It is in a good cause.' Little Sophia and her mother were banished from the country, and part of the savage sentence was that the children and their posterity should be beggars forever – which was to reckon without Him who takes beggars from the dung-hill and sets them among princes, and who will not see the righteous forsaken nor his seed begging bread. On that fatal afternoon of the day of his father's death, while children more knowing were running at the sound of the drum's frightening tattoo, it was with difficulty that little Willie Guthrie was restrained by James Cowie from playing in the streets.

With hands tied together, James Guthrie walked slowly up the High Street to the city cross. Broad-shouldered William Govan kept pace beside him. The one was nearly fifty, the other not yet out of his thirties. Greatheart and Valiant for Truth were to be seen once again upon the human scene. Soon they were upon the scaffold above the serried rows of glittering steel, and Sickerfoot, who had been offered a bishopric and had refused it, stepped forward with loving zeal to give his last message. The great crowd stood hushed to hear him say, 'I take God to record upon my soul, I would not exchange this

[1] 'die whinging on a wee pickle straw'—die groaning on his bed.

scaffold with the palace and mitre of the greatest prelate in Britain. Blessed be God who has shown mercy to me such a wretch, and has revealed His Son in me, and made me a minister of the everlasting Gospel, and that He hath deigned, in the midst of much contradiction from Satan, and the world, to seal my ministry upon the hearts of not a few of His people, and especially in the station where I was last, I mean the congregation and presbytery of Stirling. Jesus Christ is my Life and my Light, my Righteousness, my strength, and my Salvation and all my desire. Him! O Him, I do with all the strength of my soul commend to you. Bless Him, O my soul, from henceforth even forever. Lord, now lettest Thou Thy servant depart in peace for mine eyes have seen Thy salvation.' A copy of his last testimony was handed by him to a friend, for his son William when he should come to years. Then further up the ladder of death he went, exclaiming, 'Art not Thou from everlasting, O Lord my God. I shall not die but live.' And in the last seconds before he was with Christ, Mr Sickerfoot, as sure of foot and as full of faith as Joshua, lifted the napkin from his face, crying, 'The Covenants! The Covenants! They shall yet be Scotland's reviving.'

Captain William Govan, intently watching, stood by. His martial shoulders were squared. Gazing lovingly at the dangling dead minister of Christ, he thought of Calvary's Tree. 'It is sweet! It is sweet!' he cried, 'otherwise how durst I look with courage upon the corpse of him who hangs there, and smile upon these sticks and that gibbet as the very Gates of Heaven.' The hangman had him prepared. The brave soldier taking a ring from a finger, gave it to a friend, asking him to carry it to his wife, and to tell her that he died in humble confidence and found the Cross of Christ sweet, and that Christ had done all for him, and that it was by Him alone that he was justified. Someone called to him to look up to the Lord Jesus, and he smilingly said, 'He looks down and smiles at me.' As he ascended the ladder there rang out from him across the crowds these words: 'Dear friends, pledge this cup of suffering as I have done before you sin, for sin and suffering have been presented to me and I have chosen the suffering part.' The rope adjusted, he ended his witness with, 'Praise and glory be to Christ forever.' A little pause, a little prayer, the signal given, and all was over, and he too swung in the fresh summer air. Another who had magnified Christ in life, had magnified Him also in death.

Later, friends came for the bodies from which the heads had been removed. They were lovingly laid out and arranged for burial, while the heads were put up in grisly fashion above the Netherbow and West Ports.

Day by day, week by week, little feet pattered over the cobbles to the Netherbow, and young pained wondering eyes looked up at the head high above them, and returning to what home he had, little Willie Guthrie would hide himself away for hours, saying, when found, 'I've seen my faither's heid! I've seen my faither's heid!' In childhood, boyhood, and youth, in summer suns and winter storms, he saw the head that was given for Christ: 'my faither's heid!' He, too, was for Christ Jesus and the Covenants, spending much time alone in prayer, 'a serious seeker after God.' He became a scholar of excellent promise, and bent his steps after his father to a suffering ministry. But he sickened and died, and his young head was laid in the earth while the bleached skull of his father still witnessed high above the Netherbow Port of Edinburgh.

*

William Guthrie of Fenwick endeavoured to go to the execution of his valued cousin, but he was prevented from doing so by fellow-believers. They feared for his life. This truly wonderful man of God, banished from his church, died a few years later 'whinging upon a wee pickle straw.' He had a complication of diseases, and passed away in great agonies, but was uncomplaining in his suffering. He said, 'The Lord has been kind to me, notwithstanding all the evils I have done, and, I am assured, that though I should die mad, I shall die in the Lord. Blessed are the dead that die in the Lord at all times; but more especially when a flood of errors, snares, and judgments are beginning or coming on a nation, church or people.' A student under Samuel Rutherford, he received through him his call to the ministry in something of the fear and terror of the Lord. This turned to a joy and peace in believing which thrilled and filled him to the end. Only forty-five when he died, he was accounted in Scotland the greatest preacher of his day. He was the means of bringing thousands to Christ, and of establishing thousands in Christ. His lasting monument is his book, *The Christian's Great Interest*, a true spiritual classic. On this we have the word of John Owen, 'and, for a divine [taking out of his pocket a small gilt copy of Guthrie's treatise], that author I take to be one of the greatest divines that ever wrote. It is my *vade mecum*; I carry it and the Sedan New Testament still about me. I have written several folios, but there is more divinity in it than in them all.' The famous Welsh-English Puritan, in lowliness of mind, was esteeming another better than himself. But what a commendation, to get such a word from John Owen, ' a scribe every-way instructed in the mysteries of the Kingdom of God; in conversation he held up to many, in his public discourses to more, in his publications from the press to all, who were set out for the celestial Zion, the effulgent lamp of evangelical truth to guide their steps to immortal glory.'

Hugh MacKail

Hugh MacKail

Sing with me, sing with me!
Blessed spirits, sing with me;
To the Lamb our song shall be
Through a glad eternity.

Farewell, earthly morn and even,
Sun and moon and stars of heaven.
Heavenly portals ope before me;
Welcome, Christ, in all Thy glory!
Sing with me, sing with me, sing with me,
Blessed spirits, sing with me.

AMES HOGG, Covenanters' Scaffold Song

As a boy, when winter winds were howling and the rains were pouring down, I used to shiver sometimes, thinking of Covenanters, a godly nine hundred of them, in the bleak winter of 1666, straggling through my boyhood town journeying on to the Pentland Hills and tragic Rullion Green. Some of them were tied hand to hand so that the stronger among them might urge on the weaker. In pitiless weather they reached the hills, and 'cold-footed and wet-shod' stayed the night.

In all seasons the Pentland Hills are beautiful to see. But they carry nature's bounty of beauty crowned, for many of the redeemed of the Lord lie among them. In literature, the famous name linked with them is that of Robert Louis Stevenson who lived beside them. They were his own 'hills of home.' He studied much the literature of the Covenant, even

Hugh MacKail

to saying in one of his letters from far-away Samoa that his style was fashioned by Covenanter writers. 'I have been accustomed,' he writes, 'to hear refined and intelligent critics – those who know so much better what we are than we do ourselves – trace down my literary descent from all sorts of people, including Addison of whom I could never read a word. Well, low in your ear, sir, the clue was found! My style is from the Covenanting writers.' And he never forgot, and wrote, 'A Cry from Samoa.'

> *Blows the wind to-day, and the sun and the rain are flying,*
> *Blows the wind on the moors to-day, and now*
> *Where about the graves of the martyrs the whaups are crying*
>   *My heart remembers how!*
>
> *Grey recumbent tombs of the dead in desert places,*
> *Standing stones on the vacant wine-red moor,*
> *Hills of sheep, and the howes of the silent vanished races,*
>   *And winds austere and pure:*
>
> *Be it granted me to behold you again in dying,*
> *Hills of home, and to hear again the call,*
> *Hear about the graves of the martyrs the pee-wees crying,*
>   *And hear no more at all.*

At Rullion Green, among the hills, four thousand well-fed, well-armed dragoons and guards reached the haggard and homeless nine hundred, who formed up, having chosen 'never to break until He who had brought them together should break them.' Prayer was made and verses were sung from the 71st and 78th Psalms, and they strengthened one another's hands in the Lord, waiting for the onset, prepared to live Christ, or to gain greatly in death. They were of the school who know the permitted power of the devil, and in adversity rebel not against God, but bless the name of the Lord, as Job of old, neither sinning nor charging God foolishly. They believed that their sufferings were as blood-washed as their sins. 'Brother, die well, it is the last act of faith you will ever be able to do,' was the advice of one Covenanter to another, sick and dying. Their Master kept His good and best wine to the last on dark Mount Calvary, and in bringing many sons into glory He brings them this way too; and thus it was on wintry Rullion Green, the good and best wine at the last for His sake.

Once in the morning, and twice in the afternoon, those wearied countrymen beat off heavy attacks; but numbers told, and the massacre of the almost unarmed men of His Blood King Jesus, by the four to one 'belligods' of the man of blood King Charles began. In a few terrible hours was come to pass again the scripture, 'For thy sake we are killed all the day long; we are accounted as sheep for the slaughter,' and, thanks be to God, 'nay, in all these things we are more than conquerors through him that loved us.' Darkness fell on dead and wounded Psalm-singers lying all around, the reddened blades descending on others, and more escaping to be as the rabbit or the fox upon the hunting field. Here and there were groups of unkempt, half-naked prisoners who were to be kept as beasts for the shambles, in freezing winter day and night till 'the Grassmarket heard them preach from the red scaffold floor.' But whether it be on stricken field, in torture, on scaffold, or in banishment, there is no record of any who had been at Pentland ever going back from their Lord, or abjuring their Covenant made with Him. To read their testimonies is a spiritual experience never to be forgotten. They were executed in ones, twos, threes, fours, and even ten at a time. Their heads and right hands, in some cases, were sent to be put up in towns as gruesome warnings. But listen to them if you would know something of the scripture, 'He shall see of the travail of his soul, and shall be satisfied.' Here is the merchant, John Wodrow, on his dying day writing to his wife, 'O, my heart, come and see, I beseech you! I thought that I had known something of my dearest Lord before. But never was it so with me as since I came within the walls of this prison. He is without all comparison! O love, love Him! O taste and see! And that shall solve the question best.'

The soldier, Andrew Arnot, speaks from his last field of fight, 'I do account myself highly honoured to be reckoned among the witnesses of Jesus Christ, to suffer for His name, truth and cause; and this day I esteem it my glory, garland, crown and royal dignity to fill up a part of His sufferings.' The country landlord, John Neilson, heart free from his possessions, cries, 'If I had many worlds I would lay them all down, as now I do my life for Christ and His Cause.' They were exultant in their pure fervent love of the Master. Another voice spoke raucously clear in their times – that of the vile raging vices of their persecutors.

It is in the ordering of the Most High that so much has been bequeathed to us of credible writing by and for the Covenanters. And as regards the martyrs of Pentland, the fine old volume, *Naphtali, my Wrestling*, is invaluable. It was published first in 1667, the year following Pentland fight. It is no *Mein Kampf*, the struggle of a Hitler, but something so different. It is 'Naphtali,' real wrestlings of the Church of God for the kingdom of God. In it is testimony after testimony of 'grace upon grace,' and 'from glory to glory.'

It is noteworthy that about seventeen years after Rullion Green, 'The Children's Bond' should be drawn up and signed by fifteen young girls in the village of Pentland. One of these girls, Beatrice Umpherston, was only ten years of age.

It is evident that firesides in Pentland held so much of conversation about Christ and His claims that the merry minds of the young were spiritually impressed, and stilled to sober covenanting with Him. Part of the Bond reads, 'This is a Covenant between the Lord and us, to give up ourselves fully to Him, without reserve, soul and body, hearts and affections, to be His children and Him to be our God and Father, if it please the Holy Lord to send His Gospel to the land again.' And then there is their prayer, 'O Lord, give us real grace in our hearts to mind Zion's breaches, that is in such a low case this day, and make us to mourn with her, for Thou hast said, they that mourn with her in the time of her trouble shall rejoice when she rejoiceth.' No doubt, there were older, alert holy minds and devout hearts behind all this, suffering little children to come unto Him; but how heart-warming it all is, that in a mad day when men were murderously hated for reasonably loving Him, out of the mouths of some children was perfected praise.

*

One of the prisoners of Pentland who through physical weakness had not been able to be with his friends at the time of the battle, was Hugh MacKail, a scholarly young minister of twenty-five years of age. Richly gifted and very spiritual, the excellency of the power of God apparent in him, he had his treasure in an earthen vessel already breaking from a destroying consumption. He had been licensed to preach at twenty, and preached his last public sermon at twenty-one in the Kirk of St Giles, Jenny Geddes' battle-ground. There were words in that sermon some could never forget. 'The fountain,' said MacKail, 'whence violence flows may be great power which the Church cannot reach. The Scripture doth abundantly evidence that the people of God have been persecuted

29

sometimes by a Pharaoh on the throne, sometimes by a Haman in the state, and sometimes by a Judas in the Church.' There was no need of further roll-call. Pharaoh, Haman and Judas answered to their names, and he had to go into hiding from that very day. Holland was a haven to many a Covenanter, as it was to many a Puritan, and Hugh MacKail landed safely there to become more fitted to return to the unsafe land of Scotland. In 1666, he was back again ready to be offered as that cruel year closed. A hectic flush was on his cheeks, but in the mists and rains with the wanderers was also valiant Hugh MacKail. So that though not able to be in the Rullion Green fight, he was not far away, and easily taken. In due course, he appeared before a Council who seemed to think that he would tell them much. But he quietly refused to tell them anything at all, and the violent Earl of Rothes, convulsed with passion, adjudged the dying field preacher worthy of the torture of the bone and marrow mixing Boot.

Sir Walter Scott, though no reliable judge of Covenanters or their principles, drew some of his most interesting characters from Covenanting models and upon Covenanting canvas. It is to be regretted that he did not understand such admirable people, but his great books that in any way concern them, such as *The Heart of Mid-Lothian*, *Old Mortality*, and *Redgauntlet*, will be read time and again even for the Covenanters' worthy sakes. Sir Walter gives a vivid description of that cruel instrument the Boot and of its bestial torture. 'The executioner enclosed the leg and knee within the tight iron case, and then placing a wedge of the same metal between the knee and the edge of the machine, took a mallet in his hand and stood waiting for further orders. A surgeon placed himself by the other side of the prisoner's chair, bared the prisoner's arm, and applied his thumb to the pulse in order to regulate the torture according to the strength of the patient. When these preparations were made, the President glanced his eye around the Council as if to collect their suffrages, and judging from their mute signs, gave a nod to the executioner whose mallet instantly descended on the wedge, and forcing it between the knee and the iron boot, occasioned the most exquisite pain, as was evident from the flush on the brow and cheeks of the sufferer.'

A thin wasted limb of weak Hugh MacKail was placed within this hell-invented instrument, and the brutal wedge was driven home eleven savage times till the leg was smashed and pulpy, but no word of betrayal or of accusation of his brethren stained the lips of the young Covenanter. Unmoved by his afflictions, his tormentors carried him down into his dungeon to lie in painful intercession for his fellows, who outside on the gallows were dying in purity and piety for the sake of the Name and 'in the power and sweetness thereof,' in the cold, sea-tanged air of Edinburgh.

Again Hugh MacKail appeared before the men with the power of Pilate, and they in Pilate weakness condemned him to die at the Mercat Cross of Edinburgh. But he who lived in the power of a deeper death, and had the sentence of it in himself, was borne with shining face down to the Tolbooth through the large crowds who openly wept as he passed. 'Trust in God,' he called to them, 'Trust in God!' Getting a fleeting glimpse of a well-known friend, he shouted in ecstasy, 'How good is the news! Four days now until I see Jesus!' In prison a merry thrill of joy was on him, making him humorous in serious hours. Someone asking him how his crushed leg was faring; he smilingly replied that the fear of his neck was making him forget his leg. And he averred that he was less cumbered about dying than he had often been about preaching a sermon! His old minister-father came to see him, and they strengthened and comforted each other in the love of the Father and the Son.

The night before his execution he went to rest at about eleven o'clock, and his doctor-cousin, Matthew MacKail, lay by him. Doctor Matthew had gone to Archbishop Sharp for help, but 'the Judas in the Church' had not forgotten, and his answer was, 'I can do nothing.' To this the doctor replied, 'You mean, "I will do nothing."' Hugh was astir by five o'clock and awoke John Wodrow, the Glasgow merchant, who, with several other Covenanters, was to die beside him. 'Up, John,' he said, smiling, 'you and I do not look like men about to be hanged, seeing we lie so long.' But, as one having no fellowship with the throne of iniquity, earnestly he prayed, 'Lord, we come to thy throne, a place we hitherto have not been acquainted with. Earthly kings' thrones have advocates against poor men, but thy throne has Jesus Christ an Advocate for us. Our prayer this day is not to be free from death, but that we may witness before many witnesses a good confession.' His prayer was answered abundantly, and they who were seen in the weakness and scandal of the Cross showed forth the power of His resurrection.

In 1496, Savonarola preached his famous sermon, 'The Art of Dying a Good Death.' He said, 'Death is the most solemn moment of our life. Then it is that the evil one makes his last attack on us. It is as though he were always playing chess with man, and awaiting the approach of death to give checkmate. He who wins at that moment wins the battle of life.' And Girolamo Savonarola, the Evangelical Dominican, won his own battle of life through the power of life abundant in his last dread painful day, and so also did Hugh MacKail, Covenanter.

Up that eloquent path of his nation's history, the High Street of Edinburgh, the godly youth struggled along to the gallows. Crowds groaning and in tears watched him as he passed. 'He was fairer and of a more stayed countenance than ever before,' they said. Looking over the great concourse of solemn people, joyous faith suffused him, and he cried aloud in a rapture, 'So there is a greater and more solemn preparation in heaven to carry my soul to Christ's bosom.'

On the scaffold, he took out his Testimony which the great old volume, 'Naphtali,' has preserved for us. He read it to the vast crowds, 'a singularly beautiful confession of fidelity and devotion.' He had got what he said, 'a clear ray of the Majesty of the Lord.' His song of praise then lifted up into the echoes of the old city an unashamed waiting for God, a rejoicing in salvation. It was from the 31st Psalm:

> *Into Thine hands I do commit*
> *My spirit; for Thou art He,*
> *O Thou, Jehovah, God of truth,*
> *That hast redeemed me.*

Up the ladder to the rope he climbed, crying, 'I care no more to go up this ladder, and over it, than if I were going home to my father's house.' Rung by rung he called aloud, 'Every step is a degree nearer heaven.' Sitting at the top of the ladder he took out his pocket Bible, and, after addressing the crowds, he read from the last chapter of it. Standing up, the napkin was put over his face, but, lifting it, in a remarkable voice by faith inspired, he burst forth into an ecstatic offering of farewells and welcomes filled with grace and glory, a blessed, wondrous and glorious Amen of comparison.

'Now, I leave off to speak any more to creatures, and turn my speech to thee, O Lord. Now I begin my intercourse with

God which shall never be broken off. Farewell, father and mother, friends and relations! Farewell, the world and all delights! Farewell, meat and drink! Farewell, sun, moon and stars! Welcome, God and Father! Welcome, sweet Lord Jesus, Mediator of the New Covenant! Welcome, blessed Spirit of grace, God of all consolation! Welcome, glory! Welcome, eternal life! Welcome, death!' The rope tightened around his thin young neck. The watching crowds groaned dismally. And then was witnessed something surely unparalleled. 'Love never faileth,' and the great unfailing quality, unable to do any more in life, would help in death. Dr Matthew MacKail stood below the gallows, and as his martyr cousin writhed in the tautened ropes, he clasped the helpless jerking legs together and clung to them that death might come the easier and sooner. And so with Christ was Hugh MacKail 'with his sweet boyish smile.' 'And that will be my welcome,' he had said, 'the Spirit and the Bride say, Come.'

Later, the young Covenanter was laid out in the Magdalene Chapel, and dressed there for burial. Not all his fellow-martyrs were allowed this. He was laid in the earth of Greyfriars Kirkyard, where the National Covenant was signed two years before he was born. Many saw him laid away in the corner reserved for criminals, the usual bed for the Covenanter martyr from the gallows. Many had gone before and many followed. It is a much frequented sacred corner now where stands the Martyrs' Monument. The crowds go up beyond to the great and noble War Memorial high above upon the Castle Rock, but even in the snows of winter there is a well worn path to the Martyrs' graves among the wicked.

Dr Matthew MacKail missed till the end of his days his godly cousin, and in his deep mourning for him wore for as long as it could be put on the martyr's own black haircloth coat, requested by the doctor himself from the hangman.

*

Pentland Martyrs! The grand old history by Wodrow has it like this: 'I hear, most, if not all of them, left their written testimonies behind them, and it is a pity any of them are lost. Scarce the half of them are in "Naphtali." Though some of them lived long in bondage through fear of death, and others of them had some anguish of body through the wounds received in Pentland, their torture, and other pieces of ill treatment afterward, yet all of them died in great serenity and peaceful hope of salvation.'

Richard Cameron

Richard Cameron

Cameron of the Covenant stood
  And prayed the battle prayer;
  Then with his brother side by side
Took up the Cross of Christ and died
Upon the Moss of Ayr.

HENRY INGLIS, Hackston of Rathillet

SANQUHAR Town, 22 June 1680. A band of about twenty
horsemen are clattering up the High Street to the Town Cross.
People are running to see them. 'It's Richie!' they cry, 'it's
Richie Cameron! Here are the Hillmen!'

It is Richard Cameron, Lion of the Covenant, a Richard
Coeur-De-Lion, indeed, with some of the faithful remnant.
He and his brother Michael dismount. The others form a
circle about them. It is the first anniversary of the Bothwell
Brig slaughter, and for the murder of their comrades, this is
their answer – the inestimably brave Sanquhar Declaration.
In clear and solemn tones, Michael Cameron reads that they
'disown Charles Stuart, who hath been reigning, or rather
tyrannising, as we may say, on the throne of Britain these
years bygone, as having any right, title to, or interest in, the

Richard Cameron

said crown of Scotland for Government, as forfeited several years since by his perjury and breach of covenant both to God and His Kirk, and usurpation of His Crown and Royal Prerogatives therein ... As also we being under the standard of our Lord Jesus Christ, Captain of Salvation, do declare a war with such a tyrant and usurper, and all the men of his practices, as enemies to our Lord Jesus Christ, and His Cause and Covenants, and against all such as have strengthened him ... As also we disown, and, by this, resent the reception of the Duke of York, that professed Papist, as repugnant to our principles and vows to the Most High God.' That high-born wretch, the Duke of York, had sneeringly threatened to make parts of Scotland like a hunting field. From the hunted, who knew him as 'the devil's lieutenant,' this was the answer. Thomas Campbell nailed up the fearless words. Another prayer, a verse or two of a Psalm, and those men of forfeited lives disappeared among their welcoming hills.

Eight years later, the Lords Spiritual and Temporal, and the Commons of England with the Estates of Scotland, flung out King James Stuart, and put William and Mary upon the British throne. It was but a following of the brave, resolute few of the Sanquhar Declaration. As Carlyle has it, 'how many earnest rugged Cromwells, Knoxes, poor peasant Covenanters wrestling, battling for very life, in rough miry places, have to struggle, and suffer, and fall, greatly censured, bemired, before a beautiful Revolution of Eighty-Eight can step over them in official pumps and silk stockings with universal three times three!' Richard Cameron truly prophesied, 'Ours is a standard which shall overthrow the Throne of Britain.' It did.

*

To-day Northern Ireland is probably the most evangelically Christian part of Britain. This is the work of God. Had Eire known the gracious change experienced by the rest of Britain at the glorious Reformation, the history of our nation, religiously, socially and politically, would have been vastly different, and all for the better. It does not carry the light of the Reformation, the light of the Gospel. But Ulster is part of God's answer. And Ulster is a Covenanting triumph, and it was right that the last crushing blows against Stuart Romanism should be struck by Covenanter and Puritan at Londonderry, Inniskillen and the Boyne. It was in Ulster that Covenanters with Puritans settled in their godly thousands, and moved, as they termed it, 'from one bloody land to another.' The 'No Surrender' of Derry is the echo of the Covenanter cry, 'The Lord our Righteousness.' And so the blessing of God on the generations has lasted through the centuries, and is there to-day. It is not political partition only that is in Ireland. It is a fundamental partition. It is that between people and people, between the open Bible and pure evangelical faith, and a power that would draw back again into a dense darkness from which there has been a merciful deliverance. But there are two great dangers in Ulster as elsewhere in this country. These are mere nominal Protestantism and Modernism. May the people so blessedly placed inherit their heritage, winning Christ!

The present compilers of the Scottish National Dictionary have not forgotten Ulster either, and say, 'The Scottish National Dictionary deals with the vocabulary of literary and spoken Scots, including the dialects of the mainland, Orkney, Shetland and Ulster from 1700 to the present day.' Ulster is a British Covenanting triumph, and God's blessing still is there. May the people speaking the language of their fathers, speak it in the Grace of God, as their fathers most clearly did.

The United States of America, too, is a great result of the further development of the Reformation in the orderings of the Most High. It might have been settled by Spanish or Portuguese, and therefore, now been as South America, Romish, backward and dark. But in genius and constitution, in its strong depths and on its grand heights, it is a Protestant land. This is because of a people, such a people, in moral and spiritual stature incomparable, the finest expositors of Scripture ever known, the English Puritans. Carrying banished men and women, with their little children, the Mayflower was an earnest of a summer of spiritual bloom to be followed by a great harvest. The people of God suffer but to reign. Through going the way of the cross there was for them a fulfilment of the promise of the love and grace of God. And so these blood-brothers of the Covenanters went out and founded a nation like their own – lands of free men, lands of the Gospel of the grace of Christ from which to other races the message of the redeeming love of God has been taken forth unceasingly. It was King Charles Stuart that caused these people to go, but God meant it unto good. Other ships were making ready to sail, but Charles of Divine Right imperiously forbade their going. Had he but known he would have had them go, and that quickly, for two of the names of the would-be Pilgrim Colonists were Oliver Cromwell and John Hampden! Oh those days of seeming calamity to those brave and noble hearts! Those were days of the planting of the Lord. The British Commonwealth and the United States of America owe much to sufferers for His Name's sake, enduring and achieving by faith.

*

Alan Cameron, believing merchant in Falkland, Fife, had

three sons of whom Richard was the eldest. The other two, Michael and Alexander, were also believers, and followed the Covenanting banner of blue. The only daughter, Marion, was a sincere Christian woman who died at the hands of violent dragoons.

After his university days, Richard Cameron was a school-master, but he knew not the Saviour. Sometimes he listened to the here-on-earth-to-day and there-in-heaven-to-morrow field preachers, and one day, obtaining mercy and finding grace, listened unto life. His own voice was soon heard among theirs, as of a trumpet clear and certain, and thousands listened to him. He was white hot himself and had little use for the lukewarm. By his sincere example he inspired many. Even in the cold shadow of the gallows, just before they went into His Presence, there were those who testified to the blessing of God by him.

But flat, haven-affording Holland soon had to receive him, and from that easy vantage point along with other exiles he often looked back with loving longing on 'the land of blood.' While abroad godly hands were laid on his head, and he was set apart to the work to which he was surely called – the min-istry of the Gospel. After Brown, and Koelman, a Dutch minister, had lifted their hands, the great MacWard kept his upon Cameron's light brown locks saying, 'here is the head of a faithful minister and servant of Jesus Christ who shall lose the same for his Master's interest, and it shall be set up before sun and moon in the public view of the world.' A Covenanting minister's ordination!

Secretly he got back to Scotland, and soon his name was linked with the very fragrant names of Cargil, Welwood and Hall. Donald Cargill, 'blest singular Christian, faithful minis-ter and martyr'; Henry Hall of Haugh-head, 'worthy gentle-

Richard Cameron

man, martyr and partaker of Christ's sufferings'; and 'burden-
ed and temperate John Welwood,' who, seeing from his cold
den his last dawn upon his native hills, said, 'Welcome Eternal
Light, no more night or darkness for me.'

The course of Richard Cameron was as swift and bright as
that of a blazing meteor. He was fiercely hunted, but kindly
housed, and although there was a huge price on his head, there
was none that would betray him. Closely sought, he was ever
sheltered; greatly loved, and that unto death, ever with his
brother Michael by his side. His sermons were full of the warm
welcoming love of the Lord Jesus Christ for poor helpless
sinners: 'Will ye take him? Tell us what ye say! These hills
and mountains around us witness that we have offered Him to
ye this day. Angels are wondering at this offer. They stand
beholding with admiration that our Lord is giving ye such an
offer this day. They will go up to report at the Throne what is
everyone's choice.' He preached memorably from such texts
as these: *Jeremiah* 3.19, 'How shall I put thee among the
children?'; *Matthew* 11.28, 'Come unto me, all ye that labour
and are heavy laden, and I will give you rest'; *Isaiah* 32.2,
'And a man shall be as an hiding place from the wind and a
covert from the tempest'; *Isaiah* 49.24, 'Shall the prey be taken
from the mighty, or the lawful captive delivered?'; and *John*
5.40, 'And ye will not come unto me, that ye might have life.'
In the midst of this sermon, seeking to make a contract between human hearts and Christ, he fell aweeping, and crowds
wept with him, their hearts tendering to the Man of Calvary.
As was Cameron's preaching, so was his praying, and his
practising. Such as he believed what James Frazer, fellow-
sufferer in the same cause, said 'Of a Minister's Work and
Qualification': 'That which I was called to was to testify for
God, to hold forth His name and ways to the dark world, and

44

to deliver poor captives of Satan, and bring them to the glorious liberty of the children of God. This I was to make my only employment, to give myself to, and therein to be diligent, taking all occasions.' And thus he goes on, clear in his apprehension as to the greatest calling on earth, and finishing so markedly, 'and my own soul to lie at the stake to be forfeit if I failed; and this commission might have been discharged – though I had never taken a text or preached formally.' May we all be delivered from merely taking a text and preaching formally!

Then came the magnificently brave Sanquhar Declaration, and the savagely intensified hunt of the men of blood. Less than three weeks before fierce Ayrsmoss, Richard Cameron said, 'I shall be but a breakfast to the enemies shortly.' After a day of prayer, twelve days from the end, his word was, 'my body shall dung the wilderness within a fortnight.' And 'he seldom prayed in a family, or sought a blessing, or gave thanks, but he requested that he might wait with patience till the Lord's time come.' The last Sabbath of his life he spent with the dauntless veteran, Donald Cargill, and preached from Psalm 46.10, 'Be still and know that I am God.' The next Sabbath Cargill was preaching from the words, 'Know ye not that there is a great man and prince fallen this day in Israel.' It was a time of eating of the bread of affliction.

The last week of Richard Cameron's life was lived with about sixty others. Patrick Walker, the Covenanter Pedlar, the Covenanting John Bunyan, says of them in his unique record, 'they were of one heart and soul, their company and converse being so edifying and sweet, and having no certain dwelling-place they stayed together, waiting for further light in that nonsuch juncture of time.' They were somewhat armed, and about twenty of them had horses. Some may feel

Richard Cameron

that they should not have taken up arms at all. Many Covenanters themselves felt like this, believing that there was a better
testimony to be gained by suffering than by resisting. Their
own outlawed ministers and writers counselled them to be,
'as jewels surrounded by the cutting irons,' and so, 'to seal
from your own experience the sweetness of suffering for
Christ,' since 'there is an inherent glory in suffering for
Christ.' But there were many others who, while they could go
through much themselves, could not endure seeing others
subjected to the utmost miseries and cruelties, and were as
those when 'every man had his sword upon his thigh.' Whatever we feel, we cannot but love them, these rebels so glorious,
so brave for God. It was of them Delta Moir wrote:

> *We have no hearth – the ashes lie*
> *In blackness where they brightly shone;*
> *We have no home – the desert sky*
> *Our covering, earth our couch alone;*
> *We have no heritage – depriven*
> *Of these, we ask not such on earth;*
> *Our hearts are sealed; we seek in Heaven*
> *For heritage, and home and hearth.*
>
> *O Salem, city of the Saints,*
> *And holy men made perfect! we*
> *Pant for thy gates, our spirits faint*
> *Thy glorious golden streets to see;*
> *To mark the rapture that inspires*
> *The ransomed and redeemed by grace,*
> *To listen to the seraph's lyres*
> *And meet the angels face to face.*

The Lion of the Covenant spent his last night on earth at
Meadowhead Farm, the home of William Mitchell. In the
morning he washed his face and hands in an old stone trough.

On drying himself, he looked at his hands and laying them on his face, he said to Mrs Mitchell and her daughter, 'This is their last washing. I have need to make them clean, for there are many to see them.' At this Mrs Mitchell wept.

That day at about four in the afternoon, the dragoons came upon that Bible-reading band 'in the very desert place of Ayrsmoss.' The Covenanters gathered around their young leader with the horsemen on either side of those on foot. He led them in prayer, appealing three times to the Lord of Sabaoth, to 'spare the green, and take the ripe.' Looking on his younger brother, he said to him, 'Come Michael, let us fight it out to the last; for this is the day that I have longed for, to die fighting against our Lord's avowed enemies; and this is the day that we shall get the crown.' To his loved fellows he said, 'Be encouraged, all of you, to fight it out valiantly, for all of you who fall this day I see heaven's gates cast wide open to receive them.' Then, 'with eyes turned to heaven, in calm resignation they sang their last song to the God of salvation.'

The dragoons emboldened by greater numbers and better arms attacked at once. The wanderers, as was their wont, defended bravely, and David Hackston says, 'The rest of us advanced fast on the enemy, being a strong body of horse coming hard on us; whereupon, when we were joined, our horse fired first, and wounded and killed some of them, both horse and foot. Our horse advanced to their faces, and we fired on each other; I being foremost after receiving their fire, and finding the horse behind me broken I then rode in amongst them, and went out at a side without any wrong or wound. I was pursued by several, with whom I fought a good space, sometimes they following me, and sometimes I following them.' At last with a treacherous and unfair blow David

Richard Cameron

Hackston was struck down, but, he says, 'they gave us all testimony of being brave resolute men.' Nine were slain 'of that poor party that occasionally met at Ayrsmoss only for the hearing of the Gospel.' Among them had flashed to God the dauntless spirit of him known among men as the Lion of the Covenant, Richard Cameron. And Michael, the unseparable, went with him. Most escaped into the wild wide mosses. Six prisoners only were taken. These were William Manuel, John Vallance, John Pollock, David Hackston, John Malcolm, and Archibald Alison. From the severity of his wounds and from the harsh treatment he received, William Manuel died as he was being carried into the Edinburgh Tolbooth. From the same causes John Vallance died the day following. John Pollock was most cruelly treated, but in the midst of it was steadfast and cheerful, and was banished as a slave to the American Plantations with the marks of his torture still upon him.

*

From whom did the early American slaves wrested from Africa hear the Gospel? No doubt from Puritans and Quakers. But such were not fellow slaves. The former lived more in their own settlements, and the latter to their everlasting credit would not hold slaves. Whosoever got to a Quaker settlement was at once a free man. To the West Indies, Barbadoes and South Carolina many Covenanters were sent as slaves. The accounts of their tragic hell-ships make painful reading. Hundreds of these godly men and women, shipped to be sold as slaves, perished in most terrible conditions through disease, and in fearful storms were drowned miserably battened under hatches. From those who reached the Plantations black slaves heard the Gospel, and thus white-skinned slave and black rejoiced in one common Lord.

In our young years we were rightly familiar with Long-fellow's poem, beginning:

Beside the ungathered rice he lay,
His sickle in his hand,

but it is possible that it was not always an African who so lay. Now and again it may have been one who in his last visions saw not himself as if 'once more a king he strode,' but one who was back once again in fellowship among the hunted 'of one heart and one soul.'

The Negro Spirituals always have a hearing. The words of worship there united with the moving melody are a living union. But such melodies, it seems, may be sought for in vain in the negroes' own native land, Africa. Whence came they? Out of something wondrously new, the dark soul meeting with the Light of Life, Christ Jesus? Yes! And out of fellow-ship in His sufferings, and the fellowship of Christ Jesus in the slaves' sufferings. Yes, no doubt of that. But there are seeming traces of time and melody in these lovely spirituals which are reminiscent of the music of the old metrical Psalm-singing. Who can say? At any rate, these banished men and women carried the message of redeeming love to their fellow-slaves of another race.

*

The other three prisoners were executed, David Hackston being shockingly murdered upon the scaffold, and John Malcolm, and Archibald Alison were hanged. Said John Malcolm, 'let His Cause be your cause in weal and woe. O noble Cause! O noble Work! O noble Heaven! O noble Christ that makes it to be Heaven! And He is the owner of the Work! ... I lay down my life, not as an evildoer, but as a sufferer for Jesus

Richard Cameron

Christ.' Said Archibald Alison, 'What think ye of Heaven and Glory that is at the back of the Cross? The hope of this makes me look upon pale death as a lovely messenger to me. I bless the Lord for my lot this day. . . . Friends, give our Lord credit; He is aye good, but O! He is good in a day of trial, and He will be sweet company through the ages of Eternity.' Of those who escaped from Ayrsmoss, 'some wept that they died not that day, but,' says Patrick Walker, 'those eight who died on the spot with him went ripe and longing for that day and death.' The dragoons dug a pit and tumbled the dead into it, after they had cut off the head and hands of Richard Cameron, and the head of John Fowler in mistake for that of Michael Cameron. These were put into a sack to take to the blood-thirsty Council in Edinburgh. In passing through Lanark, the dragoons asked Elizabeth Hope if she would like to buy some calves' heads, and shaking the martyrs' heads out of the bag, they 'kicked them up and down the house like footballs,' so that the woman fainted.

On reaching Edinburgh, the dragoons put the heads upon halberts with the cry, 'there are the heads of traitors, rebels!' One who was there said that he 'saw them take Mr Cameron's head out of the sack; he knew it, being formerly his hearer – a man of fair complexion with his own hair, and his face very little altered, and they put a halbert in his blessed mouth out of which had proceeded many gracious words.' Robert Murray, as he delivered them to the Council, said, 'These are the head and hands that lived praying and preaching, and died praying and fighting.' And those ghouls of gore paid over the price of the blood of one who died at about the age of his Master.

Before the hangman set head and hands on the bloodstained Netherbow Port, the fingers pointing grimly upwards on either side of the head, a hero saint lying in prison was shown them. He was Alan Cameron, Covenanter. The cruel question was asked him. 'Do you know them?' 'His son's head and hands which were very fair, being a man of fair complexion like himself.' He kissed them saying, 'I know them, I know them. They are my son's, my own dear son's. It is the Lord. Good is the will of the Lord, Who cannot wrong me nor mine, but has made goodness and mercy to follow us all our days.' A prisoner, head of a broken home, the father of martyred sons and daughter! It is the answer of the more than conqueror, the sufferer in Christ, full of faith and of the Holy Ghost; and having the heart full of the power and music of the Good Shepherd Psalm:

> *Goodness and mercy all my life*
> *Shall surely follow me;*
> *And in God's house for evermore*
> *My dwelling place shall be.*

David Hackston

David Hackston

... They cut the heart from out the living man
And waved it as a flag is waved upon the battle's van;
And burned it as a beast is burned some idol to appease,
And cast the human ashes round like incense on the breeze.
And they did it in the Name of God! Where were His lightnings then,
*   That came not with consuming fire*
*   To light the everlasting pyre*
*   For these blaspheming men?*

HENRY INGLIS, Hackston of Rathillet

A GENTLEMAN of good family, related to some of the best families in the land but not in the family of God; living in the fresh bloom of early manhood, in the lovely parish of Kilmany in the Kingdom of Fife, but dead in trespasses and sins, and not in the Kingdom of God – such was David Hackston. But among the hills he went to hear the homeless wanderers preach 'Peace through the blood of His Cross,' and 'Life by His death,' and returned again to his own comfortable home a new man in Christ Jesus, sins all forgiven and having life everlasting. One now in faith with the persecuted and despised, he deliberately became one with them in practice, counting their fellowship 'greater riches,' his yea and amen one with theirs. In mountain cave and on bloody field his heart and hands were in his words, all faithful things till that cruel day when no word to man was permitted him, and of heart and hands he had none.

Covenanter, turned scented Cavalier, James Sharp, Archbishop of St Andrews, 'and the curse of God with it,' the Judas of the Covenant, was hounding to the death the people of the Lord, cutting off 'the gangrene of dissent' which was his word for the slaying of the Lord's anointed. Lives were being cut off in the dungeon, and stones cast upon them; the waters were overflowing the heads of many, and only Jesus was saying to them, 'Be strong, fear not,' when some of the hunted turned in their tracks and became hunters. And, one day, while looking for one of Sharp's confederates, they came upon the Archbishop-archkiller himself in his grand carriage with equipage driving fair for his own palace towers. And all the way from Edinburgh, too, where he had been helping to make some hell-hatched laws against the men of the cropped ears, the broken fingers and the mangled limbs. Of James Sharp, Patrick the Pedlar says, 'I have often wondered if ever the sun shone upon a man guilty of so many dreadful unheard-of acts of wickedness, attended with all aggravating circumstances to make them prodigiously heinous, except his dear brother Judas.' And here he was! The maddened band wanted to slay him at once, saying that it was God who had put him into their hands, and had scriptures to prove it so. Their leader, David Hackston, would take no part in it, saying that he himself had no call to kill the monster. So quickly they chose another leader, Hackston's brother-in-law, Balfour of Kinloch, and, galloping off, came up with the Archbishop's coach on woeful Magus Muir. Calling Sharp 'Judas' and 'murderer', they dragged him forth, and with sword and gun slew him before the eyes of his poor, shrieking, demented daughter. A few days later, Bishop Paterson, the inventor of the thumbscrews, preached his funeral sermon! But as it was a Paterson who out of hate invented the thumbscrews, so was it a Paterson, Robert Paterson, 'Old Mortality,' who, in love for the Covenanters, gave his life to follow over hill, through glen, in mosses, on mountains, and in old country church-yards, cutting the honoured martyr names afresh upon the stones above their poor remains.

And so saints killed the saint-killer, but had to be back soon again in their native air on the slopes of Mount Calvary where they were born, where they most truly lived, and best died. Many a pint of innocent blood Death was to drink because James Sharp, murder's advocate, had received his full fee from his client. That of David Hackston was to be drunk very slowly, for surely death never had crueller hands than on the day the life of this merciful man was wrung out of him.

With the scattering of the zealous band, David Hackston set off for the West Country to be with honest-hearted Cargill, to whom even in his last hours he bore witness, 'I know that the mind of God is with him.' With Donald Cárgill and others he read, prayed, fasted and sang, till the glorious Sabbath Field Meeting, which, through the too hurried attack of the cocksure dragoons, became for the Covenanters the victory of Drumclog. Claverhouse himself barely escaped with his wretched life, reserved for doom at Killiecrankie. He never forgot nor forgave Drumclog.

Tragic and pathetic Bothwell Brig came on with the fifteen thousand against the four thousand, and the righteous 'hagged and hashed, and their blood ran like water,' followed by the queues for the gallows, the tortures, and the transportations under popish captains to slavery. At Bothwell, David Hackston commanded his godly three hundred on the left side of the bridge. He appealed in vain not to be asked to retreat, and was amongst the last to leave the stricken field, escaping into the kindly folds of the Covenanters' mantle – the everlasting hills, where, with a great price set for his capture, he joined Richard Cameron and his men of one accord. One door only was open to them – the way to the Throne, by prayer or by presence. The Covenanters' colours were rightly chosen, scarlet and blue.

For a year, among the shades and mists of the glens and moors, they held sweet fellowship together, and never was there one who would betray that praying group of rebels glorious. But, on a summer day on the lone Ayrsmoss, they sang their last song to the God of their so prized salvation, and their leader Richard Cameron, the Lion of the Covenant, prayed his last prayer, crying, 'Spare the green and take the ripe,' and was gathered in as a sheaf of gold in harvest. David Hackston by his side, till Cameron fell, fought with superb horsemanship among the King's Troopers, but, his horse sticking in a bog, he dismounted to fight it out on foot with David Ramsay, an old acquaintance, when three horse-troopers coming at him from behind meanly cut him down, and he was made prisoner. 'The field was theirs,' he said, 'but they paid for it. We compelled them to give us the testimony that we were resolute and brave.'

With badly bleeding head wounds from which he thought he might die, and with a few other badly wounded sufferers, he was stripped to not even having shoes upon his feet, and set upon a barebacked horse, and taken away towards Edinburgh. Coming to Lanark, the brutal dragoons played with the hacked-off heads of Cameron and Fowler as if they had been footballs. Here also the prisoners were examined by General Tam Dalziel, the 'Muscovite Brute,' who, not getting satisfactory answers to his questions, threatened to roast Hackston alive.

The small, melancholy, shameful procession arrived near Edinburgh, and by the hangman were led into the city. Hackston, his hands tied, sat facing the tail of his white barebacked horse, with his feet tied below its belly. The other five were hauled along on some kind of iron grid or tumbril, William Manuel blessedly reaching Emmanuel's Land just as they reached the prison gates. The head of Cameron, all the while, was carried before them aloft upon a halbert, and the head of John Fowler carried in a sack by a boy.

David Hackston was immediately brought before the Council, questioned, and found to be true to Christ, the Covenant, and his fellow Covenanters, even to saying that he thought Archbishop Sharp's death to be no murder. Such is loyal fellowship – having no part in the act but a share in the sentence if need be. Some of the questions put to him he refused to answer, but requested that he might speak a little to give a testimony. This was granted, and he said, 'Ye know that youth is a folly, and I acknowledge that in my younger years I was too much carried down with the flood of it; but that inexhaustible fountain of goodness and grace of God which is free and great, hath reclaimed me, and as a firebrand hath plucked me out of the claws of Satan, and now I stand here before you as a prisoner of Jesus Christ for adhering to His Cause and interest, which has been sealed with the blood of many worthies who have suffered in these lands, and have witnessed to the truths of Christ these few years bygone. And I do own all the testimonies given by them, and desire to put in my mite among theirs, and am not only willing to seal it with my blood, but also to seal it with the sharpest tortures that you can imagine.'

In prison he wrote four letters: one to his loving sister, one to a gentlewoman of his acquaintance, and two to a Christian

David Hackston

friend. Here are a few sentences from them, 'Oh, that preachers would preach repentance, and professors would exhort one another to mourn in secret, and together, because of their sin, and with their mourning would believe, for these are very consistent together . . . It was cast up to me both at the Council and here that there were not two hundred in the nation to own our cause. I answered at both times that the Cause of Christ had been often owned by fewer . . . I think I dare not misbelieve, but when fear assaults me I think there is a voice saying to me, Fear not . . . I am frail, but Christ is strong. I have His promise of through-bearing . . . If the free grace of God be glorified in me, ought not all to praise Him?'

A few days more and he was before his merciless judges for the last time, and was asked if he had anything more to say. He answered, 'What I have said I will seal.' By reason of his wounds, they thought that he might die if tortured, so they asked him to sit down to receive his sentence. He did so willingly, but told them that they were all murderers. Sentence of death was then passed upon him, and what a death sentence! It is clear from the old records that the manner of his execution was framed before his last trial. It stands against his judges till this day. Here is the sentence in all its stark savagery: 'That his body be drawn backward on a hurdle to the Cross of Edinburgh; that there be a high scaffold erected a little above the Cross, where in the first place his right hand is to be struck off, and after some time his left hand; that he is to be hanged up and cut down alive, his bowels to be taken out, and his heart to be shown by the hangman to the people; then his heart and his bowels to be burned in a fire prepared for that purpose on the scaffold; that afterward his head be cut off, and his body divided into four quarters, his head to be fixed on the Netherbow, one of his quarters with both his hands to be affixed at

St. Andrews, another quarter at Glasgow, a third at Leith, a fourth at Burntisland; that none presume to be in mourning for him, nor any coffin brought; that no person be suffered to be on the scaffold with him save the two bailies, the executioner and his servants; that he be allowed to pray to God Almighty, but not to speak to the people; that the heads of Cameron and Fowler be affixed on the Netherbow; that Hackston's and Cameron's heads be affixed on higher poles than the rest.'

Already dying from his ghastly wounds, he was led away to suffer. While great crowds looked on, there was done upon him by the hangman a gross, painful barbarity not mentioned in his sentence. Then he endured with firmness and patience the cutting off of his hands, but, the hangman having taken such a long time to hack off his right hand, he asked that his left hand might be taken off at the joint, which was done. With a pulley he was then pulled to the top of the gallows, and when choked a little was let down alive. The hangman then with a sharp knife opened his breast, and putting in his hand pulled out his heart. It fell upon the scaffold and moved there. The hangman picked it up on the point of his knife, and, carrying it around the scaffold, he showed it to the people saying, 'Here is the heart of a traitor.' Patrick Walker says that it fluttered upon the knife. The rest of the sentence was duly carried out. The free grace of God was glorified in David Hackston, so that whoever thinks of him must think of his Lord and Saviour, Jesus Christ, too.

About a fortnight later two of his fellow-soldier peasant saints followed him. John Malcolm and Archibald Alison by the rope glorified God in the Grassmarket. Said John Malcolm, 'I bless the Lord that ever He made choice of me, who was a miserable sinner, to lay down my life for His Cause.'

David Hackston

Said Archibald Alison, 'For my part I am glad that He calls me away after this manner, for which I desire with my soul to bless Him for His kindness to me in taking this method, and this way, with such a wretched sinner as I am, who deserves nothing, nothing but wrath and only wrath.' So they joined their fellow-soldier in Christ, David Hackston, with him to get

> *a standing there and place*
> *Among the beams, which crown the face*
> *Of Him, who died to part*
> *Sin and my heart.*

John Brown

John Brown

The child on the moss she laid
And she stretched the cold limbs of the dead,
And drew the eyelid's shade,
And bound the corpse's shattered head,
And shrouded the martyr in his plaid;
And where the dead and living slept,
Sat in the wilderness and wept.

HENRY INGLIS, The Death of John Brown

THE simple name of John Brown is familiar and famous. Literature, history and religion all witness that more than one 'John Brown's body lies a-mouldering in his grave while his soul goes marching on.' Several Covenanting martyrs bore this honoured name, and, among his godly namesakes, John Brown of Priesthill has a humble, gracious place. Though but a peasant believer, he was a type of manhood at its best, full orbed in Christ, ascending the hill of the Lord with clean hands and a pure heart.

Like many another Covenanter, he came from the Shire of Ayr, the land of Burns, by him famed in lovely song as long as the world lasts; of Montgomery, the Moravian singer of heavenly songs; the land of Murdoch of coal-gas discovery; of MacAdam who has done so much for our roads; of Baird,

John Brown

discoverer of television; and of Fleming, discoverer of penicillin. Ayrshire is the old Land of Kyle, famous for its Lollard preaching and staunch adherence to Reformation principles. Dear to its exiles, even when within sight of the better country, one of them said to old Adam Sanderson, after the cruel day of Rullion Green where he had received his death wounds, 'Bury me within sight of my Ayrshire Hills.' The Pentland farmer saw him pass into the presence of his dearly loved Saviour, 'free frae the toil and the moil and the mirk, and the tyrant's cursed pride,' and, taking up the poor broken clay upon his back, he carried the nameless lad and buried him on a ridge from where one can see the dim outline of the low Ayrshire Hills.

John Brown was the very close friend of both Richard Cameron, the Lion of the Covenant, and of Alexander Peden, 'Puir Auld Sandy,' the Prophet of the Covenant. Cameron he looked upon as the very voice of God for his generation, and quoted him as such; while the fellowship on earth of Peden was to him a taste of the joys of the world to come. When Brown fell, Peden referred to him as 'a clear shining light, the greatest Christian I ever conversed with.' He had married the Covenanter to Isabel Weir in 1682, and after the simple Puritan ceremony had said to Isabel, 'Ye have a good man to be your husband, but ye will not enjoy him long; prize his company, and keep linen by you to be his winding sheet, for ye will need it when ye are not looking for it, and it will be a bloody one.' A Covenanting wedding! The Covenanter's deepest joys ever carried the shadow of the Cross.

John Brown of Priesthill was poor. Till the day he died he never owned much more than twenty sheep and a cow. His small crofting cottage is now no more. On every side stretch miles upon miles of melancholy moorlands with the heather creeping lovingly around his memorial stone. He was buried where he fell, just outside his own door. One need but stand in the silence there to hear again the humble little family at worship, and John Brown singing his last psalm, the psalm of the 'dull misty morning.' It sings in one's heart till it fills earth and sky with its music, till it blends and is lost in the greatest psalm of all – the song of the redeemed in the great day of triumph – 'Worthy is the Lamb that was slain.'

By all accounts he was rarely gifted, and carried a brilliant intellect yielded to Christ. He had his own rustic school of theology, and his classes were attended by youths from miles around. Three of these class members sealed their testimonies with their blood, and their leader had often times to flee. An impediment in his speech had made him give up the thought of being a Covenanting minister, but here was his own Bible School where he taught youth to resist unto blood, striving against sin. In the summer time they held their classes in the sheepfold, and in the winter they sat around the peat fire in the kitchen. We rightly look upon John Brown of Priesthill as being one of our first founders of Bible Classes and Sunday Schools. O that eternity might stage for us some of the holy scenes of time! Who would not like to see the Bible School at Priesthill with John Brown in his class of peasant students, candidates for martyrdom?

How well one can imagine them going over Walter Smith's 'Twenty-Two Steps of Defection,' and 'Rules for Society Meetings,' and praying God to help them to follow out faithfully, with all other members of the United Societies, the teaching set down therein by that enlightened soul! How greatly at heart the Covenanters had the Church, the Jew, and the unreached heathen. What would they have done had they had the present opportunity? Though hunted like wild beasts, the Spirit of God testifies that they had the mind of Christ. Here is a small part out of their Rules for Society Meetings: 'As it is the undoubted duty of all to pray for the coming of Christ's kingdom, so all that love our Lord Jesus Christ in sincerity, and know what it is to bow a knee in good earnest, will long and pray for the out-making of the Gospel promises to His Church in the latter days, that King Christ would go out upon the white horse of the Gospel, conquering and to conquer, and make a conquest of the travail of His soul, that it may be sounded that the kingdoms of the world are become His, and His Name called upon from the rising of the sun to its going down.

'1 That the old casten of Israel would never be forgotten, especially in these meetings. That the promised day of their ingrafting might be hastened; and that dead weight of blood removed off them, that their fathers took upon them and upon their children, that have sunk them down to hell, upwards of seventeen hundred years.

'2 That the Lord's written and preached word may be sent with power to enlighten the poor pagan world, living in black perishing darkness without Christ and the knowledge of His Name . . . that they would love, sympathize, and pray for one another in secret, and in their families who have them, and weep when any member weeps, and rejoice with all such as are joined in this society communion which is the strictest of all communions; and before they go to their meetings everyone would be importunate with the Lord to go with them and meet with them, that it may be for the better and not for the worse, and with all such meetings.'

So this moving paper runs on to its close, 'Rules and Directions anent Private Christian Meetings for Prayer and Conference to Mutual Edification, and to the Right Management of the Same.' With other four martyrs, the writer of it, Walter Smith, was hanged at the Cross of Edinburgh, 27 July 1681. The other four were Donald Cargill, James Boig, William Cuthil, and William Thomson – 'and all their five heads hashed and hagged off upon the scaffold by the common man's Bloody Axe: the first three heads fixed upon the Netherbow-port, and the last two upon the West-port.'

Says Patrick Walker, speaking of Cargill, 'He wrote that by virtue of the mercies of God and merits of Christ, he had a conscience as quiet and calm as if he had never sinned,' and continues, 'When he came to the scaffold and foot of the ladder he blessed the Lord with uplifted hands that he was thus near the crown; and when setting his foot upon the ladder to go up to embrace the bloody rope, he said, 'The Lord knows I go up this ladder with less fear, confusion or perturbation of mind, than ever I entered a pulpit to preach.' He was first turned over. 'Mr Smith, as he did cleave to him in love and unity in life, so he died with his face upon his breast.' So went to Heaven, young, twenty-six years old, 'singular worthy, and faithful-unto-death Mr Walter Smith,' with a heart filled for world-wide evangelization.

*

The year 1685 was a terrible year in a terrible era. The Killing Time reeked reddest then. The author of *Robinson Crusoe*, Daniel Defoe, one of the most painstaking and sympathetic writers on the Covenanters, 'fixes on the barbarities of this year to support his opinion that the Scottish persecution was worse than that of the Roman Emperors and Popish Inquisitors.' It was also from this year that Lord Macaulay selected his history of a single fortnight to show the horrors of government under a Stuart king. Long is the roll of the names of the

John Brown

martyrs – the lashed to the hooks, the burned by the match, the redhot iron branded, the starved to death, the bone mangled and crushed, the earclipped, the banished, the wounded and torn by bullet and knife. But as the horrors are bestial and brutal, so are the testimonies tender and spirit quickening. The Covenanters died praying and praising. While their persecutors lived in sin, they prepared themselves for Heaven, deeming themselves blessed forever because blessed of the Lord.

In April of that year, the hawks that harry were searching hill, glen, moss and moor, looking for two shepherds of the flocks, the man Peden and the boy Renwick. One night Peden arrived at the holy haven of Priesthill, stayed the night, and went away again very early in the morning, saying in his prophetic way, 'It is a fearful morning, a dark misty morning.' Between five and six next morning, after family worship, John Brown with his young nephew, John Browning, went out to cut some peats. They had not long been gone when, in the midst of a dark and thick mist, Claverhouse with three troops of horse looking for Peden came upon them. They ran, but were caught and brought back to Priesthill for cruel cross-examination. The bare-footed lad was shamefully treated. Claverhouse in a letter relates his own cruelty to the boy. He was questioned much, sentenced to death, ordered to pray, and faced the firing squad. Bloody Clavers then reprieved him, saying that he would hand him over to justice, and that he would make an appeal for him. Captain Drummond was to have charge of him. Alas! it seems from history that Drummond hanged the laddie with the bare feet. The word of Clavers was like himself – just Clavers.

Priesthill was ransacked and so-called treasonable papers were found. Brown was questioned. His stammering disappeared, and he answered **every** question so solidly and distinctly that Claverhouse asked his base guides if ever they had heard him preach. 'No, no,' they said, 'he was never a preacher.' 'Well,' said he, 'if he has never preached, much has he prayed in his time. Go to your prayers,' he shouted, 'for you shall immediately die.' The peasant went to his knees and began to pray, but three times Claverhouse interrupted him, and then completely stopped him as John Brown interceded, asking God to spare a remnant. 'I gave you leave to pray,' he bawled, 'and you have begun to preach.' The Covenanter turned upon his knees, 'Sir,' he said, 'you know neither the nature of preaching nor praying that calls this preaching,' and, looking to God, finished his last prayer. 'Take good-bye of your wife and children,' said 'the pitiful creature,' Bonnie Dundee – the Ugly, man of blood. Isabel Brown was standing by with her child in her arms, and another child of John Brown's first wife by her side. He came to her saying, 'Now, Isabel, the day is come that I told you would come when I spoke to you first of marrying me.' She said, 'Indeed, John, I can willingly part with you.' 'That is all I desire,' he replied. 'I have no more to do but to die. I have been in happy case to meet with death for so many years.' He kissed her and his children, saying that he wished Blood-bought and Gospel-promised blessings to be multiplied upon them, and Claverhouse roughly broke in, ordering six dragoons to shoot him. As he stood before them their hearts were moved; they lowered their muskets and refused to fire. But the killer of many unbelted his pistol, and hastily walking up to John Brown, placed it to his head, and blew his brains out, scattering them upon the ground. Looking at his ghastly work with a sardonic smile, he turned to Isabel saying, 'What do you think of your fine husband now'? and through her sad tears she bravely answered, 'I ever thought much good of him, and more than

John Brown

ever now.' 'It were but justice to lay you beside him,' he returned. Said she, 'If you were permitted, I doubt not but your cruelty would go that length. But then, how will ye answer to God for this morning's work'? Arrogantly, he blustered, 'To man I can be answerable. And as for God, I shall take Him into my own hand!' He then mounted his horse and haughtily rode off at the head of his troops. He later confessed that if he gave himself liberty to think of it, he could never forget John Brown's prayer.

Isabel Brown set her child upon the ground, gathered up her husband's brains, tied up his head, straightened his body, and covering it with a plaid, sat down and wept. Thus was she found by widow Jean Brown, whose own husband and two sons had been slain in the same great cause.

About ten miles away Peden had been in the fields all night. Very early in the morning he called at a country cottage where lived a praying family named Muirhead, and asking them for fellowship in prayer, he began to pour out his heart in melting crying to God. 'Lord,' he cried with all the poignant pathos of the helpless wanderer, 'Lord, when wilt thou avenge Brown's blood! Oh, let Brown's blood be precious in thy sight.' John Muirhead enquired from him what he meant. 'What do I mean,' said this strange unusual saint of God, 'I mean that Claverhouse has been at the Priesthill, and has cruelly murdered John Brown. His corpse is lying at the end of his house, his poor wife sitting by it, with not a soul to speak comfortably to her.'

It was on a May morning, the first day of summer in the Killing Time, that Isabel Weir offered up the priceless jewel of her life, John Brown her husband. He went swiftly to company he had often longed for, where he would be much at home. She lived on in brave, godly, covenanting widowhood, bringing up her children, succouring the godly, and comforting the mourner with the comfort wherewith she had been comforted of God.

*

The Book of the Intricacies of My Heart: the *Memoirs of James Frazer, Covenanter*, is not as well known as *Grace Abounding to the Chief of Sinners*, but maybe it ought to be. Himself a sufferer, he testifies to the consolations and comforts of the Lord. Says he, 'The greatest consolations do attend the greatest tribulations, 2 *Corinthians* 1.5–6. The first brunt of the cross is saddest and sharpest; no affliction for the present seemeth joyous but grievous. Great outward troubles, whether personal or on public accounts, quicken and revive our apprehensions of eternity, and always do us good, though not alike good to all, nor so sensibly. Yet no cross but we get some good of it. I found it very hard to appear before councils and carry rightly. We seek rather to save ourselves in any lawful way than to give testimony for Christ.' And he closes his great memoirs in a way that reaches us all till He comes, 'There is a large allowance for sufferers for righteousness; but many live not upon their allowance, and therefore look so ill upon it.'

Margaret MacLachlan
and Margaret Wilson

Margaret MacLachlan and Margaret Wilson

Long had they loved as Christians love –
Those two so soon to die,
And each the other greeted first,
With weeping silently.
The matron wept that that young life
So timelessly must cease;
The maiden that that honoured head
Must not go down in peace.

But soon, O soon, it passed away
The coward thought and base,
And each looked humbly, thankfully,
Into the other's face.
'Mother, He rules the awful sea
With all its waters wild.'
'The many waters are His Voice
Of love to thee, my child.'

HARRIET STUART MENTEITH, The Martyrs of Wigton

LIKE some other Protestant institutions many of our Orange Lodges have lost their pristine spiritual power. Without the Spirit, the reading of the Scriptures and the saying of prayers can be lifeless formalities. There remains but a round of social fellowship and a name. Yet an Orange Walk is a stirring sight! The fluttering banners, trimmed in their ribbons of orange and blue, bring to mind the scripture, 'terrible as an army with banners.' And as the banner, 'Solway Martyrs,' is carried past with its vivid picture of the faithful Margarets dying amid the swirling waters, what heart has not felt thankful for what they died to win – freedom to worship God.

*

Before a very savage court, at Wigtown, 13 April 1685, stood

Margaret MacLachlan and Margaret Wilson

four female prisoners. They all had refused Prelacy and the oath of Abjuration, which latter made its swearer own the Church of God to be a department of the state. Their indictment was for rebellion, attending of field meetings, and meetings for worship within doors – twenty of each! Finding them guilty, Grierson of Lagg, a violent persecutor of the Covenanters, ordered that they should receive sentence while on their knees. They refused to kneel, but were brutally forced to, and were held down while sentences were pronounced upon them: Margaret MacLachlan, widow, seventy years of age, to die by drowning; Margaret Maxwell, serving maid, twenty years of age, to be flogged publicly through the streets of Wigtown three days in succession, and to stand each of these days for an hour in the stocks; Margaret Wilson, farmer's daughter, eighteen years of age, to die by drowning; Agnes Wilson, sister of Margaret, thirteen years of age, her father, Gilbert Wilson, to pay £100 bond for her.

Margaret MacLachlan was of a manner of life Christlike and very highly esteemed by her fellow-Christians. Patrick Walker says, 'Those of her intimates said to me that she was a Christian of deep exercise through most of her life, and of high attainments and great experiences in the ways of godliness.' She was much harassed by the persecutors, and one day, while she was upon her knees worshipping God with her family around her, a party of dragoons arrived, arrested her, and put her in prison, where she suffered much from want of food, fire and bed. She had not even light to read the Holy Scriptures. All her record is in these words, 'Faithful unto death.'

Patrick the Pedlar tells us also that when Margaret Maxwell was an old woman he talked with her, and she told him, 'she was then a prisoner with them and expected the same sentence, but she was ordained to be scourged through the town of Wigtown by the hand of the common hangman three days successively, and to stand each day one hour in juggs [stocks]. All which was done. But such was the cruelty of these days that all who retained anything of humanity toward their fellow-creatures were often shocked from their passivity into showing open abhorrence for such barbarity; so that all the three days that the foresaid Margaret was punished and exposed, there was scarce one open door or window to be seen in the town of Wigtown, and no boys or girls looking on. The officers and hangman enquiring if they should shorten the hour, she said, "No! let the clock go on." She was neither wearied nor ashamed. The hangman was very tender to her.'

Margaret and Agnes Wilson, daughters of rich Gilbert Wilson, farmer in Glenvernock, had with their brother Tom, of sixteen years of age, refused to conform to vain religion. Searched for, they fled and lived among the wild mountains, bogs and caves, youthful, vagrant, holy things. Their parents were charged on their highest peril that they should neither house them, give food to them, speak to them nor see them. The country people were ordered by law to pursue them even as did the rude soldiery.

Their parents were yet to suffer much for the godliness of their children. For several years at a time, as many as a hundred soldiers were quartered on them. Heavy fines were exacted, and courts were imposed, meaning a once-a-week horse journey of many miles which went on for three years, and Gilbert Wilson died at last in utter poverty. His wife was supported and cared for by friends, and when Tom returned from soldiering in the army of William of Orange, there was nothing left to return to.

Margaret MacLachlan and Margaret Wilson

During February, the two girls left Tom among the snows of the mountains and came down secretly to see some friends in Wigtown, where someone asked them to drink the King's health. That they could not do, they said, for it was not warranted by Scripture, and belied Christian moderation. Thus they were recognized, arrested and thrust into prison in the Thieves Hole, as if they had been ferocious criminals. There they lay until their trial on 13 April, when, with the widow and serving-lass, they heard their sentences, and judged it an honour to suffer for their Saviour's sake.

Gilbert Wilson paid the heavy bond for his little Agnes, and set off on horseback to Edinburgh with an appeal for Margaret. But, by the time he returned, the sad tragedy had taken place, and she was where there is 'no more sea.'

*

John Brown 'won Hame,' on May morning. Next day, beneath the early summer sun, these two ladies of the Covenant, Margaret Wilson and Margaret MacLachlan, were wrestling in their cruel heavy swellings of Jordan. They were summer and winter in the glorious cause, Margaret of the flaxen hair, and Margaret of the grey. From the darksome prisonhouse, the soldiers took them to the banks of the Blednoch Burn which fills with Solway from the sea when the swift-running tide comes in. Two long wooden stakes had been fixed deeply in the bed of the burn. The farther out one, nearer the oncoming waves, was for mother Margaret; and the other, nearer to the land, was for Margaret the maid.

We never read of any word the old saint spoke. It appears that, sick at heart and disappointed with madly cruel humanity, she turned to unending communion with the Lord. 'It is needless to speak to that damned old bitch,' they rudely cried, 'let her go to hell,' and they tied her roughly fast to her leafless but fruitful tree. So came the hungry waters up and up, every wave splashing death, until she was choking in their cold, cold grasp. As she struggled, before she became a poor limp thing lying in the swirling flood, they said to young Margaret, 'What do you think of her now?' 'Think! I see Christ wrestling there,' said she. 'Think ye that we are sufferers? No; it is Christ in us, for He sends none a warfare at their own charges.'

The waters were now around her, and she began to sing a plaintive melody she had often sung among the hills when the fellowship of the hunted worshipped God. In it the young heart communed with the Most High. It was Psalm 25 from the seventh verse:

> *My sins and faults of youth*
> *Do thou, O Lord, forget:*
> *After thy mercy think on me,*
> *And for thy goodness great.*
> *God good and upright is:*
> *The way he'll sinners show;*
> *The meek in judgment he will guide*
> *And make his path to know.*

To the Covenanter the Bible was the visible earnest of the New Jerusalem, 'that great city, the holy Jerusalem, descending out of heaven from God, having the glory of God: and her light was like unto a stone most precious, even like a jasper stone, clear as crystal.' Her treasure with her, Margaret Wilson opened it up for the last time, to see the precious jewels there. She read aloud from the eighth chapter of Romans, in full assurance of faith of the glory soon to be. 'Whom He justified them he also glorified'; and, convinced of His bearing her through to His praise, 'we are more than conquerors through him that loved us. For I am persuaded that neither death nor life, nor angels, nor principalities, nor powers, nor things present, nor things to come, nor height, nor depth, nor any other creature, shall be able to separate us from the love of God, which is in Christ Jesus our Lord.' The cold waves dashed over her head. Loosely tied, the soldiers pulled her out of the water, and when she could speak they asked her to do what the Covenanter could not do – pray for the King, 'as he is supreme over all persons and causes, ecclesiastic as well as civil,' a blasphemous usurping of the prerogative of Christ as Head of the Church, an arrogant claim which no Covenanter would admit. 'Pray for the King,' they cried! She murmured that she wished the salvation of all men, and the damnation of none. They dashed her under the water and pulled her out again. 'Oh, Margaret, say it,' pleaded some. 'Lord, give him repentance, forgiveness and salvation, if it be Thy holy will,' she whispered. Grierson of Lagg, in wild, impatient passion cried, 'Damned bitch, we do not want such prayers. Tender her the oaths.' She groaned, 'No! No! no sinful oaths for me. I am one of Christ's children. Let me go.' And they brutally flung her back into the waters, where she died a virgin martyr of eighteen summers.

Their dear dust lies in Wigtown Old Churchyard. It is but a few yards from where they died. The dust of several other martyred Covenanters lies near them.

*

Among the Covenanters, the roll of greatly suffering women who laboured in the Gospel is a very large one. They truly loved Him, and loved not their lives unto the death. And as they comported themselves in the prisons, in the slaveships and in the waters, so did they also upon the scaffold.

Isabel Alison and Marion Harvie, two young hearts alive

unto God and dead to the world, were tried together upon the one indictment, and executed on the same day together, 26 January 1681, after singing the 23rd Psalm and, a little later, the 84th Psalm, to the mellowed tune of Martyrs, resplendent with the dew of the field, the love of the heart, and the blood of the gallows tree. By every word and act they glorified their Saviour; and their written and spoken testimonies minister grace. Wrote Isabel, 'What shall I say to the commendation of Christ and His Cross? I bless the Lord He has made my prison a palace to me. And what am I that He should have dealt thus with me? I have looked greedy-like to such a lot as this, but still thought it was too high for me when I saw how vile I was.' Wrote Marion, 'Now farewell, lovely and sweet Scriptures, which were aye my comfort in the midst of all my difficulties! Farewell, faith! Farewell, hope! Farewell, wanderers, who have been comfortable to my soul, in the hearing of them commend Christ's love! Farewell, brethren! Farewell, sisters! Farewell, Christian acquaintances! Farewell, sun, moon and stars! And, now, welcome my lovely, heartsome Christ Jesus, into whose hands I commit my spirit throughout all eternity. I may say, few and evil have the days of the years of my life been, I being about twenty years of age.'

The simple word of appreciation for Isabel and Marion from Alexander Peden was, 'they were twa honest worthy lassies.' Honesty and honour are of one heart, an old pilgrim power like faith, and hope, and love. 'They were twa honest worthy lassies' and in them grace reigned.

> *Yonder in joy the sheaves we bring,*
> *Whose seed was sown on earth in tears;*
> *There in our Father's house we sing*
> *The song too sweet for mortal ears.*

Margaret MacLachlan and Margaret Wilson

Sorrow and sighing all are past,
And pain and death are fled at last,
There with the Lamb of God we dwell.
He leads us to the crystal river,
He wipes away all tears forever;
What there is ours no tongue can tell.

John Nisbet

John Nisbet

and no more
The assembled people dared in face of day,
To worship God, or even at the dead
Of night, save when the wintry storms raged fierce,
And thunder peals compelled the men of blood
To couch within their dens; then, dauntlessly,
The scattered few would meet, in some deep dell
By rock o'er canopied, to hear the voice,
Their faithful pastor's voice; he by the gleam
Of sheeted lightning, ope'd the Sacred Book,
And words of comfort spake.

JAMES GRAHAM, The Sabbath

T H E night had been dark and long, but when Wycliffe, the Morning Star of the Reformation, arose, there were watchers also in Scotland who hastened to his rising, and gathered gold in his shining. One of these was Murdoch Nisbet, of Kyle, who, greatly enriched in the free grace of God, left the miserable hovel of Popery for large room in the Family of God among the first British Protestants, the Lollards.

Threatening storm clouds gathering, he went overseas, taking with him a highly treasured manuscript New Testament, and returned when a brighter day was promised. But the storms broke again on all not sheltered by Rome, and Kennedy and Russell, two of Murdoch Nisbet's colleagues, perished in the hell-heated martyr fires of Glasgow.

Murdoch dug deep, and built a vault below his house where

John Nisbet

he lived a life of prayer. Here he continually read his hand-written New Testament and taught its great doctrines to learners in Christ. With them he eventually went forth boldly preaching the Gospel. Thus, till glory, continued Murdoch Nisbet.

To Alexander, his son both in the flesh and in the Spirit, he left his precious manuscript. Alexander lived in its power, and left it to his son James, a man much taught of the Lord, and greatly strengthened by his help-meet, Janet Gibson, whose praise in the churches continued through many years. She died young, leaving two children, Mary and John, who saw their father through his long widowed days bend low over the Word of God, and then go home. To big, strong, broad-shouldered John, soldier of the Thirty Years' War, passed the loved manuscript New Testament.

On his return from the wars, John Nisbet married Margaret Law. They settled down comfortably enough until 1661 when King Charles and his counterfeit Protestants drew aside from Reformation principles, whereupon John and Margaret were found among the godly band who renewed their covenant with God in *the* Covenant.

The Killing Time came on and the military might of Britain prowled the land with a devouring mouth given to it by the devil. Once more, John Nisbet was a soldier. But he had no bright gay uniform now; just the Lowland peasant hodden grey sometimes splashed with living red. No proudly mar-shalled ranks, nor blast of enlivening trumpets now, but the thinned ranks of the wanderers and their speaking to one another in the silences by imitated call of beast and bird. Such could but win one battle, but it the real one – the victory of faith.

Came Pentland Fight cold and bitter, and while many fell

to die, he fell to live with seventeen ugly wounds, from which it took him a year to recover. Stripped naked, he was left for dead upon the field, but, in the chilly wet November night, he crawled away to safety.

Drumclog and Bothwell Battles followed, where he got the testimony that he comported himself as a valiant soldier and as a true Christian. From the Bothwell defeat he got away, and the vindictive dragoons, not finding him, made homeless his wife and children, who began their wanderings 'in deserts, and in mountains, and in dens and caves of the earth.' But as Margaret Law was at the beginning of her sore suffering when the steel was pointed at her breast, and the pistol was at the ready, so was she till the end, faithful. For four years she and her children battled on, and on a cold December day she sank low among the straw of a sheep cot never to rise again. Eight days she lay, her children by her, and then fell asleep in Jesus. Strangers to the daytime came out with the nightshadows, laid her in the earth, and faded away again. News came to John Nisbet, and, arriving eight days later, he entered the 'sheep cot where was no light or fire but that of a candle, no bed but that of straw, no stool but the ground to sit on.' Friends were putting his little daughter in her rude coffin. Stooping down, he kissed her tenderly, saying, 'Religion does not make us void of natural affection, but we should be sure it runs in the channel of sanctified submission to the will of God, of whom we have our being.' Turning to a corner where two of his sons lay in a burning fever, he spoke to them but they did not know him. He groaned saying, 'Naked came I into this world and naked I must go out of it. The Lord is making my passage easy.' One of the friends said to him, 'I hope ye know who hath done this?' But the Covenanter's eyes were ever on God, and John Nisbet answered as one whose thought was taken up in profound and inaccessible mystery, passing all second causes, 'I know that He hath done it that makes all things work together for the good of them who love Him and keep His Way, even He who first loved us, and this is my comfort. Also it doth comfort me very much that my wife whom ye have already buried out of my sight bears the mouth that never bade me do that that might hurt my conscience, notwithstanding of all the troubles she met with on my account. On the contrary, when I was telling her at any time, I dare not do such and such a thing, she would have said, "Well then, see that ye do it not, come of me and my bairns what will. God lives, we need not be afraid, and if ye, they and I were once fairly in Emmanuel's Land, we would be richly made up." I bless God who gave me such a wife, and I bless Him that He hath taken her again.' To Stonehouse Kirkyard they carried his dear child, he bearing her head all the way, and at midnight she was laid in close upon her mother's breast. Quickly he went off again into hiding. The troops got notice of his being about but they found neither him, his sons, nor the graves of his womenfolk.

For about two years more he was among the hillmen and wrote his 'Large Testimony to Truth,' in case he was killed in the fields. A huge price was offered for his capture, and blood-drinkers were eager to get it.

So came the day when he and three others met together for prayer and business, and, as wrote his son James, 'it pleased God they were seen.' Forty dragoons came upon them and a fierce fight took place in a byre. Shots all spent, with the stocks of their muskets they fought the soldiers, till, the commander ordering the place to be set ablaze, they came out into the open and fought bravely there. The leader of the dragoons, Captain Robert Nisbet, was a relative of Covenanter John Nisbet, and, seeing the possibility of a rich prize, he called for taking him alive. John Nisbet had seven severe wounds, and the other three were badly wounded, but they fought on till all of them were beaten to the ground and made prisoners. Redcoat Nisbet, gloating over his captives in front of his relation's face, shot his brave fellow-Covenanters, Peter Gemmall, George Woodburn, and John Fergushill. Speaking to John Nisbet, the butcher asked what he now thought of himself and his circumstances. Nisbet replied, 'I think as well of Christ and His Cause as ever, and not all the worse for what I suffer. Only I grieve and think myself at a loss that I am left in time when my three dear brethren are gone to heaven, whom ye have wickedly murdered.' He was told that he would have a worse death, and he was taken away on his painful journey to Edinburgh where at his trials he made noble answer for his faith. He told his judges there that he was more afraid to lie than to die, and that he was as willing to give his life as they were to take it. Sentence of death being pronounced upon him, he blessed and praised God that he was counted worthy to suffer for Christ's sake.

He was in prison very cruelly treated, having a load of irons on him of seven stone weight, and not able to move much because of his terrible wounds. But all the time he was filled with inexpressible joy and continually witnessed to strong inward assurance and assistance from the Holy Spirit. He testified, 'It has pleased Him to give me such real impression of unspeakable glory as without constant and immediate supports from the Giver will certainly overwhelm me. This frail tabernacle is not able to hold up under what I now feel.'

A few days before he was hanged, he was so transported while at worship with other prisoners that he called aloud in prayer, 'O for Friday! O for Friday! O Lord, give patience to wait Thy appointed time! O give strength to bear up under

Thy sweet, sweet Presence! If Thou, O glorious, Thou the Chief of ten thousands, the eternal wonder, and admiration of angels and redeemed saints put not to me more strength, this weak clay vessel will rend in pieces under the unspeakably glorious manifestations of Thy rich grace and matchless, matchless Presence!'

In prison, he wrote his Last and Dying Testimony. It is one of the most remarkable of Covenanter Testimonies. It is written truly by one who knew that he 'had been lying dying and rotting in his blood-red sins, and One had passed by and in His love and life said, Live, Live.' It is a pæan of praise and closes in this moving harmony, 'Be not afraid at His sweet, lovely and desirable cross, for although I have not been able because of my wounds to lift up or lay down my head, but as I was helped, yet I was never in better case all my life. He has not given me one challenge since I came to prison, for anything less or more; but on the contrary He has so wonderfully shined on me with the sense of His redeeming, strengthening, assisting, supporting, through-bearing, pardoning and reconciling love, grace and mercy, that my soul doth long to be freed of bodily infirmities and earthly organs, that so I may flee to His Royal Palace even the Heavenly Habitation of my God, where I am sure of a crown put on my head, and a palm put in my hand, and a new song in my mouth, even the song of Moses and of the Lamb, that so I may bless, praise, magnify and extol Him for what He hath done to me and for me. Wherefore I bid farewell to all my dear fellow-sufferers for the testimony of Jesus, who are wandering in dens and caves. Farewell, my children, study holiness in all your ways, and praise the Lord for what He hath done for me, and tell all my Christian friends to praise Him on my account. Farewell, sweet Bible, and wanderings and contendings for truth. Welcome, death. Welcome, the City of my God where I shall see Him and be enabled to serve Him eternally with full freedom. Welcome, blessed company, the angels and spirits of just men made perfect. But above all, welcome, welcome, welcome, our glorious and alone God, Father, Son and Holy Ghost; into Thy hands I commit my spirit for Thou art worthy. Amen.'

His greatly-longed-for Friday came. He was taken before the Council and out from them into the thronged city streets where the crowds watched the stalwart figure of the many wounds, 'eyes lifted up to Heaven, his face shining visibly.' There was a bright happiness about him from communion with God. He spoke little to the people till he came down the hill 'of the sanctified bends of the Bow' into the Grassmarket, and saw his gallows tree. Jumping up upon the scaffold, he called aloud, 'my soul doth magnify the Lord! my soul doth magnify the Lord! I have longed these sixteen years to seal the precious cause and interest of precious Christ with my blood. And now, now He hath answered and granted my request, and has left me no more ado but to come here and pour forth my last prayers, sing forth my last praise to Him in time on this sweet and desirable scaffold, mount that ladder, and then I shall quickly get home to my Father's House, see, enjoy, serve and sing forth the praises of my glorious Redeemer, for evermore world without end.'

He then spoke to the assembled crowds, earnestly urging them to hide in Christ from swift-coming judgments, and the soldiers thundered upon their drums to drown out his voice. His choice of Scripture was the eighth of Romans, the choice of many another dying Covenanter. Did he read from the manuscript New Testament? He prayed with deep spiritual understanding in a loud clear voice, and sang the first six verses of the 34th Psalm:

John Nisbet

God will I bless all times: His praise
My mouth shall still express.
My soul shall boast in God: the meek
Shall hear with joyfulness.

Extol the Lord with me; let us
Exalt His name together.
I sought the Lord; He heard, and did
Me from all fears deliver.

And so died, aged fifty-eight, the gallant and godly John Nisbet, 'with the full assurance of his interest in the ever-blessed Lord Jesus Christ.'

That same day, 4 December 1685, another brave heart was stilled in Edward Marshall of Kaemuir. He too died with the glow of salvation bright upon him – 'out of love to Christ,' he wrote, 'and His Covenanted work.' He left a wife and seven children. Which is to come first? The work of God, or wife and family? With our own, with one another, and with all concerned there is the utmost need of patience and of tenderness. In Sir Walter Scott's *Journal*, Moore is quoted as having said, 'More mean things have been done in this world under the shelter of "wife and children" than under any pretext worldly-mindedness can resort to.' So are we beset with peril in the most blessed place of earthly life – home. 'As an angel of light,' says Paul, 'as an angel of light!' So may come the angel of the bottomless pit, and not be so easily recognized by the warm fireside's kindly glow, as in many another place.

But Edward Marshall won through and commended his 'wife and seven children to the good guiding of my God who hath hitherto protected me: for He has promised to be a husband to the widow, and a father to the fatherless, providing they will walk in His ways, and keep His commandments.

Now, I commend my soul to God, who hath preserved me hitherto and who unexpectedly has singled me out to suffer for Him, who am the unworthiest of all sinners, and I never thought that He should have so highly privileged me, as to account me worthy to give a testimony for Him, though sometimes it entered into my thoughts, "Oh, if I should be called to it!" ' And the call came, and having the spirit of the Bride he was ready.

His testimony has the glorious echo in it of John Cochran, shoemaker, who two years earlier, being hanged with two other Covenanters, and leaving a wife and six children, testified as he thought of the hardship endured, 'That was no discouragement to me; for when the storm blew hardest, the smiles of my Lord were at the sweetest. It is a matter of rejoicing unto me to think how my Lord hath passed by many a tall cedar, and hath laid His love upon a poor bramble bush, the like of me.'

> *God's saints are shining lights; who stays*
> *Here long must pass*
> *O'er dark hills, swift streams, and steep ways*
> *As smooth as glass;*
> *But these all night,*
> *Like candles shed*
> *Their beams, and light*
> *Us into bed.*

James Renwick

James Renwick

The Word of God
By Cameron thundered, or by Renwick poured
In gentle stream; then rose the song, the loud
Acclaim of praise; the wheeling plover ceased
Her plaint; the solitary place was glad,
And on the distant cairns, the watcher's ear
Caught doubtfully at times the breeze-borne note.

JAMES GRAHAM, The Sabbath

ONE day in a secondhand bookshop, not far from Grey-friars Kirkyard, I picked up an old calf-bound volume, and on opening it happily found that it was 'A choice Collection of very valuable Prefaces, Lectures, and Sermons Preached upon the Mountains and Muirs of Scotland in the Hottest Time of the late Persecution, by that Faithful Minister and Martyr of Jesus Christ, The Reverend James Renwick.' I saw that it had been owned, in 1780, by one of my own name. It cost me a shilling! What a prize!

In the foreword, one writes of James Renwick: 'He travelled with great pain and diligence through the mosses, muirs and mountains, displaying the banner of the Gospel faithfully, in the dark cold stormy nights as well as in the day time, breaking the Bread of Life to his hearers. Often times, he had no better place of retirement to consult his Master's mind than a cold glen, cleugh, den or caves of the earth – and that for the unfeigned love he had to Christ, His Cause and persecuted people.

'He was hotly pursued and persecuted by open enemies, grievously reproached by many false lies and slanders spread against him by false brethren, backslidden professors, and such as ran into right-hand extremes. Under all which he gave many convincing evidences that he esteemed the reproach of Christ greater riches than all the treasures in the world.

'The more he was afflicted the more the work of the Lord grew in his hand. The archers sorely wounded him but his bow abode in strength. The Lord made him immovable not only to believe, but to suffer patiently for His sake, and, at the last, He honoured him to seal with his blood those truths which he taught to others.

'His martyrdom was at the Grassmarket of Edinburgh on 17 February 1688. He was then twenty-six years old. He was lovely and pleasant in his life, and he obtained such a good report at his death as will make his memory sweet and savoury to the generations of the righteous while sun and moon endure.'

It is a tenderly wise saying, 'He that taketh away pity from his friend forsaketh the fear of the Lord.' In this old foreword, it is as the foreword of William Penn to the Journal of George Fox, full of friendship's pity from knowledge of the truth, the voice of ungrudging love: 'Many sons have done excellently in their day, dear George, but thou, thou excellest them all.'

*

In James Renwick culminated the fierce, great and grand battle of one hundred and fifty years for Scotland's spiritual freedom. It was the supply of the Spirit of God that brought forth man after man strong in the Lord and in the power of His might, to finish stupendously in this man as living, able, and ready, as though he were the first and only in the glorious Cause. Young, vigorous, zealous, tender, of delicate touch, and holy, he was a thrilling compelling figure carrying in him the convincing strength of the early Reformers, winning at the last the commendation, 'He was of old Knox's principles,' and 'stedfast, unmovable, always abounding in the work of the Lord,' as his fellow-Covenanters gone before, with their victory of faith on him, the bright promise of the church set free. To read what he wrote and what was written of him by his contemporaries is to know that in him it was the Lord God continuing to appear for His people. Even now

> *At mention of his name, a fragrance rare*
> *Of Lily of the Valley sweet,*
> *Of Rose of Sharon fair,*
> *Perfumes the heart.*

He was born to Christ-trusting weavers in the clachan of Moniaive, among the hills of Glencairn, a child of faith, coming when all the other children of Andrew and Elizabeth Renwick had died. Whilst Andrew had been content that his little ones were with Christ, Elizabeth had cried unto the Lord, and was heard of Him for another male child. James came, and was given back to the Giver, and his parents were glad when they saw him at a very early age begin to pray and to read the Scriptures. He was a child of tender conscience, and, endowed with natural gifts, he grew in favour with folks around, so that, after his time at the Parish School, friends got him to Edinburgh to prepare him for the University where he kept his faith, triumphed over temptations, and qualified for his

Master of Arts degree which he refused to accept because the Oath of Allegiance was required from him.

The Oath of Allegiance was required from all in positions of authority and from all who were to be so placed. It virtually made the King a Pope. But in the Covenanter's glorious hope was no Pope, be he Pope or King! They knew that nothing could be given in exchange for their souls and so reigned as kings in such knowledge. A Christ-enlightened conscience to them was of greater power than all kings and governments whatsoever and altogether. The hard foolish heart of the Oath was, 'I acknowledge my said Sovereign only Supreme Governor of this Kingdom over all persons and in all causes . . . I shall never decline His Majesty's Power and Jurisdiction as I shall answer to God.' Such was part of the Divine Right of Kings supported by those who held a great deal of right for themselves while it meant position and money. Charles II 'only Supreme Governor!' Charles II! He was as brutal as Genghis Khan, as immoral as a Greek god, and as false as the religion he died in when Priest Huddleston, the Benedictine, was brought into the death chamber and, according to York, Charles 'made his confession to him, was reconciled, received the blessed sacrament, had the extreme unction . . . and died unconcerned as became a good Christian.' A good Christian! It was the false word for the false hooded Protestant at the last. And York attested two papers, saying that he had found them in the King's strong box – papers written by the hand of Charles, and the words occur in them, 'One church . . . and none can be that church but that which is called the Roman Catholic Church.' A good Christian? No! Rome and romance both claim him, but he was no witness for Christ Jesus.

Renwick remained in Edinburgh and saw martyrdoms there. He told Patrick Walker, the Pedlar, that he watched the public murder of Robert Garnock, of Stirling, in youth full flowered in Christ, 'esteemed by all to be a singular Christian, of deep exercise, high attainments, great knowledge and experience in the ways of the Lord.' With him died other four of like love of Christ, all happy by Christ's death destroying him that had the power of death. Renwick with some friends lifted their mutilated bodies and buried them, and took down from some of the city gates, heads, hands and other parts of martyrs' bodies. Also before this, he saw Cargill die with the shameful, bloody rope round his neck, and his hands uplifted, as he had been wont to pray. Other four died with him, by every expression saying, as wrote one of them, 'Welcome, cross; welcome, gallows; welcome, Christ.' That was a great day for Renwick, for it was then that his heart was knit by Christ Jesus into one with the wanderers. He never forgot the moving sight of old, dead blest Cargill hanging on the gibbet, and the head of young, scholarly and saintly Walter Smith reclining on his breast. Writes Patrick Walker: 'As he did cleave to him in love and unity in life, so he died with his face upon his breast.'

Towards the end of 1681, there was great need of the remnant binding up its ranks, and a drawing closer together of all the praying and fellowship societies in the land, and James Renwick with eager zest gave himself to work for God and His people in these, called the United Societies. They chose four young men to go abroad to study for their ministry and James Renwick was one of them. He went to Gröningen and was a pupil of the famous John à Marck who recommended that he be ordained before Renwick was six months with him, and he was soon back again in the land he loved. 'I think,' said he, that if the Lord could be tied to any place it is to the moors and mosses of Scotland.' And he wrote, 'I think that within a little there shall not be a moss or a mountain in the West of Scotland which shall not be flowered with martyrs.'

He was present at Darmead at the General Meeting of the United Societies, 3 October 1683, and satisfied all there as to his testimonies in Christ and His Cause. A call was then given to him to the ministry in the United Societies, which he agreed to accept, and he spoke to those assembled from *Isaiah* 40.1–8, and from *Isaiah* 26.20. And so he became to many of them, Mr James Renwick, the only minister of Christ in all Scotland; all others were hirelings who cared not for His sheep, and they were His sheep, of this they were sure. They were the people of His pasture and the sheep of His hand, and well knew the voice of the Shepherd. At the time of the Darmead Assembly, there were in the United Societies upwards of eighty societies with a very widely scattered but one-hearted non-Baal membership of seven thousand men, besides women and children. Among these he had his ministry, churchless, homeless and hunted, but loved. Oh, so loved! by hearts that best can love, those in whom the love of God is shed abroad by the Holy Ghost. They were enemies of God who referred to him derisively as 'James Renwick, Field-preacher, Rebel, Vagrant!'

Then followed his four years of wonderful work – each year worth seven. Preaching, teaching, organizing, counselling, formulating Papers and Declarations, he was the strength in defence, the power for attack, in one of the most important spiritual battles of world history. All was headed up in young James Renwick. Like Hugh MacKail, he was none too strong in body, but even the strongest would have failed in the way he had to go. Writing to his dear friend, Sir Robert Hamilton, he says in one of his beautiful letters, 'My business was never so weighty, so multiplied, and so ill to be guided to my apprehensions, as it hath been this year; and my body was never so frail. Excessive travel, night wanderings, unseasonable sleep and diet, and frequent preaching in all seasons of weather, especially in the night, have so debilitated me that I am often incapable for any work, I fall into fits of swooning and fainting. When I use means for my recovery I find it some ways effectual; but my desire to the work, and the necessity and importunity of the people prompts me to do more than my natural strength will allow, and to undertake such toilsome business as casts my body down again. I mention not this through any anxiety, quarrelling or discontent, but to show you my condition in this respect. I may say that under all my frailties and distempers I find great peace and sweetness in reflecting upon the occasion thereof; it is a part of my glory and joy to bear such infirmities, contracted through my poor and small labour in my Master's vineyard.' Whoso reads the Letters of Samuel Rutherford should also read the Letters o James Renwick. There is the man, his heart, his life and love, all visible. Of these letters, J. King Hewison says, 'The letters of this simple peasant, for grace, elegance of diction, and delicacy of feeling, are comparable with the best productions of his age, and afford a striking contrast to the miserable, vulgar, ill-spelled compositions of the fashionable hacksters who hunted the rebels to death.'

In the year 1685, King James summoned a Scots Parliament, and ignorant nobles with a great deal of choler, bad taste and bad temper made acts, a bevy of them, as Satan-faced and Satan-voiced as were ever made, giving his Romish Majesty armies of men between sixteen and sixty years of age, and abundance of supplies: a pseudo-Protestantism for Scotland [and heavy fines to be extracted from the husbands of wives who would not listen to the timber-tuned preachers[1] of it];

[1] Having no ear or voice for the music of true Protestantism.

treason to be among the godly, and saying Yea and Amen to the Covenants of 1638 and 1643; sentence of death, and the taking away of everything belonging to hearers and preachers at field meetings – and a lot more besides, all having one dire aim, to exterminate for ever the 'new sect sprung up among us from the dunghill, the very dregs of the people . . . whose idol is that accursed paper, the Covenant.'

King Robert Bruce, a few hundred years before Covenant times, when was signed, at Arbroath, the Independence of Scotland, wrote that as long as one hundred Scotsmen were alive their country would be defended. It was a noble vow in a noble cause. In Blackgannoch Moss, in the end of May, 1685, two hundred Scotsmen gathered – two hundred Christian Scotsmen. A nobler vow they made in a nobler Cause. They were there from their shelters in the mosses, caves, haystacks, dykesides and churchyards, and their leader was James Renwick, slim and pale with the gentleness of Christ upon him, but with no timidity of compliance. By faith that Parliament, 'without the camp bearing His reproach,' had a bruised Satan under their feet.

The two hundred Covenanters at Blackgannoch 'bearing in their bodies the marks of the Lord Jesus' are an interesting sight. Let a cruel and bloody king following his fathers, and a mad blood-lusting Parliament legislate murder for him, there was no fear in the faith of those Christ-thrilled souls, and they triumphed over every power that could be brought against them. They overcame their world by faith. At Blackgannoch, they framed their Protestation and Declaration, for ever to be known as the 'Second Declaration of Sanquhar.' That little town was not very far away, and they marched to it as good, purposeful Richard Cameron, the Lion of the Covenant, and his brave hearts had done a few years before, and there again –

oh, the blessed againness of the things of faith! – by the Psalm, the prayer, and the determined fixing of the Declaration at the Town Cross. King, Parliament, Church and Army, all heard afresh and clear that 'the bleeding remnant' would obey God rather than men, and live, and die if need be, for the Crown Rights of their Redeemer. It is quite evident that Renwick both wrote the Second Declaration of Sanquhar and proclaimed it: 'Let King Jesus reign, and all His enemies be scattered.'

*

Wrote Paul to Timothy, when about to die, 'Take Mark and bring him with thee, for he is profitable to me for the ministry.' It was not always so. There was a time when Paul had little use for the young man who 'went not with them to the work.' But there came about a blessed change, and such an one as 'Paul the aged' would have with him in the Roman prison, John Mark. And old Alexander Peden, the Prophet of the Covenant, 'in deaths oft,' was truly dying now in his cave, and he must see the young man Renwick whom he had never met, but of whom he had believed some hard things. By all his afflictions, Puir Auld Sandie was hastening on to the joy of his Lord, and he sent for James Renwick. Patrick Walker tells the fine old story. 'He said to James Wilson, that from the time he drank in these false reports, and followed these unhappy advices, it had not been with him as formerly; and when he was a-dying, he sent for Mr Renwick, who hasted to him and found him lying in very low circumstances, overgrown with hair, and few to take care of him, as he never took much care of his body, and seldom unclothed himself, or went to bed. When Mr James came in, he raised himself upon his bed, leaning upon his elbow with his head upon his hand, and said,

"Sir, are ye the Mr James Renwick that there is so much noise about?" He answered, "Father, my name is James Renwick; but I have given the world no ground to make any noise about me; for I have espoused no new principle or practice, but what our Reformers and Covenanters maintained." "Well, sir," said Mr Peden, "turn about your back," which he did in his condescending temper. Mr Peden said, "I think your legs too small, and your shoulders too narrow, to take on the whole Church of Scotland on your back; sit down, sir, and give me an account of your conversion, and of your call to the ministry, of your principles, and the grounds of your taking such singular courses, in withdrawing from all other ministers;" which Mr Renwick did in a distinct manner; of the Lord's way of dealing with him from his infancy, and of three mornings successive in some retired place in the King's Park, where he used to frequent before he went abroad, where he got very signal manifestations and confirmations of his call to the ministry, and got the same renewed in Holland a little before he came off; with a distinct short account of his grounds upon which he contended against tyranny and defections, and kept up an active testimony against all the evils of that day. When ended, Mr Peden said, "Ye have answered me to my soul's satisfaction, and I am very sorry that I should have believed any such ill reports of you, which have not only quenched my love to you, and marred my sympathy with you, but made me express myself too bitterly against you, for which I have sadly smarted. But, sir, ere you go you must pray for me, for I am old, and going to leave the world;" which he did with more than ordinary enlargement; when ended, he took him by the hand, and drew him to him, and kissed him and said, "Sir, I find you a faithful servant to your Master; go on in a single dependence upon the Lord, and ye will win honestly through and cleanly off the stage, when many others that hold their head high will fall and lie in the mire, and make foul hands and garments"; then prayed, that the Lord might spirit, strengthen, support and comfort him in all duties and difficulties. James Wilson was witness to this, and James Nisbet, who then lived in that countryside, could have asserted the truth of this.'

They never met again. Peden, ever a phantom to the troopers, evaded them to the last, but forty days after he was buried, they dug him up as he said they would, and hung him on a gallows, and out of contempt for him, reburied him at the gallows foot. But his lowly bed became the last resting place for the folks of Cumnock Town.

> Think ! no more in the old graveyard,
> Will anyone bury his dead!
> They carry them high to the Gallows Hill
> And lay them there at his head.

And two shot Covenanters, David Dunn and Simon Paterson, lie by his side.

*

Renwick hastened on, Christ the fruit of his labour, and knowing, as Peden had said, 'Grace is young glory!' Making full proof of his ministry, he showed himself as given to the Lord and unto His people, by the will of God. A hundred escapes he had, remarkable deliverances, but the inevitable often cast its shadow, and, one winter night in Edinburgh, he lodged in the house of a friend, and was found there in the early morning. He tried to escape but was badly injured by a cruel blow which made him fall down several times as he tried to run, and 'the dog Renwick' was taken. Put in irons, he there called upon the Lord to carry him through his sufferings to His praise. On being examined, with apostolic boldness he testified

calmly and clearly to his preaching of Christ and Him crucified. Two little note books were found in his clothes, and in
them were the heads of two sermons lately preached – 'these
treasonable sermons.' His indictment makes us shake our
heads with very shame as we read of the childishness, and the
barbaric heathen savagery of 'the powers that be; ordained by
God' – the stewards of God for the good of society, and yet
the cursers of it. It is a short indictment making out Renwick
to be an utter villain and traitor. 'You, the said Mr James Renwick, having shaken off all fear of God, and respect and
regard to his majesty's authority and laws; and having entered
yourself into the society of some rebels of most damnable and
pernicious principles and disloyal practices, you took upon
you to be a preacher to those traitors and became so desperate
a villain that you did openly and frequently preach in the
fields,' and so on, and so on. It is a relief to turn from it all, to
him, the prisoner of Christ Jesus.

His father dead, his prayerful mother, a sword piercing her
own soul also, came to see him when she was allowed to. The
compassion of the Good Shepherd in him, he told her that he
was troubled at being taken away from his widely scattered
flocks but that he was trusting the Chief Shepherd to meet
their need, and that he was sure he had fed them wisely and
led them in the right way. One time, on her asking him how
he fared, he told her that he was very well, but that since his
last examination by his judges, he could not get to prayer at all.
On seeing her concern, he smiled and added, 'I can hardly get
praying, I am so taken up in praising, and am ravished with
the joy of the Lord.' He was reigning in Christ, reigning in the
grace of God, and the Lord to him was 'as the light of the
morning, when the sun riseth, even a morning without clouds,
as the tender grass springing out of the earth by clear shining

after rain.' She confessed to him, 'O James, sometimes I think that I shall faint in the day of battle. How shall I look up to your head and hands set up upon the city gates? I have so much of self I shall not be able to endure it.' But he, used to looking at things unseen, assured her that this would never be. 'I have willingly parted with my life,' said he, 'and have humbly sought of the Lord to bind them up from going any further, and I am much persuaded they shall not be permitted to go any further.' And so it was that he who when free among the hills was sometimes troubled lest he should fail his Lord when brought to judgment, was now, when bound and in prison, dwelling in a peaceable habitation, kept by the power of God. Very few of those who bore the reproach of Christ were allowed to see him. To them by his every attitude and word he said, 'I press toward the mark for the prize of the high calling of God in Christ Jesus.'

Early in February 1688, the dark dawning of a bright year, he was again brought into court and his indictment again read to him. He was asked if he adhered to his former confession, and did he acknowledge all that was in his libel. Having no advocate, he counted himself happy to be permitted to speak for himself, with earnest dignity standing to all that he had formerly admitted. But he objected to the sharp part in the indictment which said that he had cast off all fear of God. 'That I deny,' he said, 'for it is because I fear to offend God, and violate His law, that I am here standing ready to be condemned.' Asked if he owned King James to be his lawful Sovereign, he answered, 'No! I own all authority that has its prescriptions and limitations from the Word of God; but I cannot own this usurper as lawful king, seeing both by the Word of God such a one is incapable to bear rule, and also by the ancient laws of the kingdom which admit none to the

James Renwick

Crown of Scotland until he swear to defend the Protestant Religion, which a man of his profession cannot do.' He was then asked, 'How can you deny him to be king? Is he not the late king's brother? Has the late king any children lawfully begotten? Is James not successor of Charles by Act of Parliament?' All these questions he answered very straightforwardly, saying in his summing-up of James, 'that from the Word of God that ought to be the rule of all laws, or from the ancient laws of the Kingdom, it could not be shown that he had, or ever could have, any right to be king.'

The question as to whether Charles II had any children lawfully begotten or not was a pitiful one to ask from such a man as James Renwick. He was as pure, as fresh and as clean in his life, as Charles had been corrupt and vile. Children lawfully begotten? No! Charles II had no children lawfully begotten. The answer of James Renwick was, 'What children he had I do not know.' But the cruel truth is out long ago. Of his children unlawfully begotten, thirteen grew up to manhood and womanhood.

Renwick was then asked if he owned and had taught that it was unlawful to pay cesses and taxes to his majesty. His answer was that it was unlawful so to do, adding, 'would it have been thought lawful for the Jews in the days of Nebuchadnezzar to have brought every one a coal to augment the flame for the furnace, to devour the three children, if so they had been required by the tyrant? And how can it be lawful, either to oppress people for not bowing to the idols the king sets up, or for their brethren to contribute what may help forward their oppression on that account?' And so it went on, question and answer, the lone witness for Christ, no man standing by him, being carried through and over the fleshly minds of the strongly-placed, salvationless men. As became the saint that he was, he told them that he would give his blood as a testimony as readily as give his word. And they having the same urge as had some of old when by wicked hands they crucified and slew the Holy and the Just, sentenced him to die. But one or two of them showed conscience; one, Somerville, actually running away when Renwick directed some speech to them. He said that he trembled to think to take away the life of such a pious-like man though he should lose his whole estate. The young Covenanter was sentenced to die in the Grassmarket the following Friday and was asked by Linlithgow if he desired longer time. He answered, 'It is all one to me. If it is protracted it is welcome. If it is shortened it is welcome. My Master's time is the best.' He was then taken back to prison and his execution deferred till 17 February. This favour was granted in the hope that he would recant, but he said that he had never asked for such leniency, and stood firm, winning the testimony that 'he was of Old Knox's principles.'

John Bunyan's Greatheart tells us of Mr Fearing, 'I took notice of what was very remarkable; the water of that river was lower this time than ever I saw it in all my life. So he went over at last, not much above wet shod.' And that is lovely. James Renwick was not Mr Fearing, but he knew that Someone would measure out the waters for him too, and his cry of faith was, 'Our Jordan is before us; it will be very deep, but it will not be very broad.' He lived by the faith of the Son of God, 'Away with poverty-stricken sense,' he said, 'which ever constructs God's heart to be as His face. Faith is a noble thing; it soars high, it can read love in God's heart when His face frowns.' The Cross of Christ was his joy, 'I have found Christ's Cross sweet and lovely, I have had many joyful hours and not a fearful thought since I came hither.'

Though treated kindly in prison, he was not allowed fellowship with any known Covenanter. Others came of varied theological and religious colours whose hues pleased a King and state who were actually colour-blind as far as religion was concerned. They all felt the false thrill of being on the side of power and pitied the young man whose views of Scripture made him hold to principles for which he was losing his life. Thumbscrew Bishop Paterson came asking, 'Do you think that none can be saved but those of your principles? Will you kill yourself with your own hand, seeing that you can have your life upon easy terms?' But when the heart is given the word is readily found in the mouth, and it was with no uncertainty in the worthwhileness of his devotion that Renwick made answer, 'I never said or thought that none could be saved but such as were of my principles, but I am of the opinion that those truths for which I suffer are sufficient grounds to suffer upon.'

In gown and canonical habit, one named MacNaught got entrance to him. Renwick told him that he did not like his coat; it was a bad badge. But he conversed with him. Frequently, priests of Rome came and with every visit left more and more convinced that the young Covenanter was certainly a hell-going heretic. And the jailors had a saying among them, 'Be-gone, as Renwick said to the priests!' And so it was that though his Word-of-Life hearers in the shadowed glens would listen to him no more, his mission continued to the last amongst those whose zeal made them persecute the Church of God. To them it was given to see a young man count all things but loss for the excellency of the knowledge of Christ Jesus his Lord.

Three days before he was hanged, he was again brought before the Council and there witnessed cheerfully that he was glad that he was counted worthy to suffer shame for Christ.

He told a friend who kindly asked how he was, that he was very well but that he expected to be much better in a few days. To his mother he said that he saw need for his suffering at this time, believing that his death would do far more good than his life would have done were he to live many years.

Writing was denied to him while in the condemned cell, even as friends were. He had begun to write a testimony but pen, ink and paper had been taken from him. Yet how it was it is not known, the night before his execution he had a testimony written, and got it out. It is fully given in the grand old book, *The Cloud of Witnesses*, where it can be read and re-read with spiritual profit. It carries the power of the Covenanter, that of the Cross. It begins on earth and finishes in heaven. Here is the latter part of it, to his loved fellows. 'He has strengthened me to brave man and face death, and I am now longing for the joyful hour of my dissolution, and there is nothing in the world that I am sorry to leave but you; but I go to better company, and so I must take my leave of you all. Farewell, beloved sufferers, and followers of the Lamb; farewell, Christian intimates; farewell, Christian and comfortable mother and sisters; farewell, sweet societies; farewell, desirable general meetings; farewell, night wanderings, cold and weariness for Christ; farewell, sweet Bible and preaching of the Gospel; farewell, sun, moon and stars, and all sublunary things; farewell, conflicts with a body of sin and death. Welcome, scaffold for precious Christ; welcome, heavenly Jerusalem; welcome, innumerable company of angels; welcome, general assembly and church of the first-born; welcome, crown of glory, white robes and song of Moses and the Lamb; and, above all, Welcome, O Thou blessed Trinity and one God! O eternal One! I commit my soul into Thy eternal rest.'

He wrote also 'A Letter to His Christian Friends.' It speaks of loyalty to God and to his fellow-Covenanters. Here are short parts of it. 'Yesterday I was cast into a deep exercise, and made to dwell under the impression of the dreadfulness of everything that might grieve the Spirit of God. I found sin to be more bitter than death, and one hour's hiding of God's face more insupportable . . . They also urged me, upon pain of torture to tell where our societies were, who kept our general correspondence, and where they were kept. I answered, though they should torture me, which was contrary to all law after sentence of death, I would give them no further notice than the books gave.' His two little books! 'I was, moreover, threatened to tell my haunts and quarters, but I refused to make known to them any such thing; so I was returned to prison. Such exercises as I had were very needful to me for such a trial; and I would rather endure what they could do unto me, than have dishonoured Christ, offended you, and brought you into trouble. But I hope, within less than three days, to be without the reach of all temptations. Now I have no more to say – Farewell again in our Blessed Lord Jesus.'

*

On 17 February 1688, out of the cold darkness of a wintry night, the light of day struggled, to lie a grey leaden sea above the hills and valleys of Edinburgh. The waking thought of thousands that chill morning was of James Renwick that day in faith to die, not yet receiving the promise of the Church of Christ set free. By the end of the year there would be freedom and light, but the day of his testimony and death was a day of chains and darkness, and he in the grim blackness of it all fearing no evil.

Helpers in sorrow and the sorrow-laden are early astir,

and James Renwick's mother and young sisters were soon on their anxious way to the prison house to eat a little with him, and to worship. When the young Covenanter returned thanks that morning, he said, 'O Lord, thou hast brought me within two hours of eternity, and this is no matter of terror to me, more than if I were to lie down in a bed of roses; nay, through grace, to thy praise, I may say I never had the fear of death, since I came to this prison; but from the place where I was taken, I could have gone very composedly to the scaffold. O! how can I contain this, to be within two hours of the crown of glory.'

Responsibility and experience take from us fancied knowledge, and in place of it reveal reality. So James Renwick with a trial of faith more precious than of perishing gold was well fitted to speak to his loved ones on life and death. He said to them, 'Death is the king of terrors but not to me now, as it was some times in my hidings; but now let us be glad and rejoice, for the marriage of the Lamb is come, and His wife hath made herself ready. Would ever I have thought that the fear of suffering and of death could be so taken from me? What shall I say to it? "It is the doing of the Lord and marvellous in our eyes." I have many times counted the cost of following Christ but never thought it would be so easy, and now who knows the honour and happiness of that? "He that confesses me before men, him will I confess before my Father." ' His mother wept, and with disciplined tenderness he said to her, 'Remember, mother, they who love anyone better than they do Christ Jesus are not worthy of Him. Rejoice with me that I am going to my Father to obtain the enjoyment of what eye hath not seen, nor ear heard, neither hath entered into the heart of man the things that God hath prepared for them that love Him!'

James Renwick

God so loved us that He gave His only begotten Son for us upon the Cross. The Son of God so loved us that He left the presence of His Father to agonize in the lonely darkness of the Cross, crying, 'My God, my God, why hast thou forsaken me?' Such is the love of the Father and of the Son for mankind. So James Renwick was following in the steps of the example given. His hating himself and his loved ones, his forsaking all, and his taking up of the cross, were all born out of the love of God — the hate that draws its life from love.

He went to prayer that lifted into loving praise, to heart-breaking, loving intercession for the afflicted of the Lord, His Own, and then up again into praise, the heart filled with the everlasting song, 'Worthy is the Lamb that was slain.' The drums thundered for the guard, and officials nervously made for their posts. The crowds began to surge along the narrow streets, the godly praying and the loving weeping. The martyr smiled. They were his drums now, not theirs. All things were his. In triumphant joy, he shouted, 'Yonder is the welcome warning to my marriage; the Bridegroom is coming; I am ready, I am ready.'

Love is ever on the Cross or standing near it, albeit weeping. If it lapses, it may follow afar off and broken-heartedly repent. But it never sits down and coldly watches Him there. And so it was as the last leader of the Wanderers and his loved ones broke apart from one another for the last time; the cross was taken by them all and held fast by love; and he turned towards the gallows by way of the Low Council House, where he was asked to say what he had to say, and to pray what he had to pray, for when he should get to the scaffold no word would be permitted him either to man or to God. The drums would drum, and drum, and drum again, until the only sound in all the world would be the sound of drums, and the only sight his death. The Covenanter answered that he had prepared nothing either to pray or to say, but that the Holy Spirit would be His guide. It is the answer of the prepared spirit. They asked him if he would like one of their ministers to be with him. He said, 'No! if I would have had any of them for my counsellors or comforters, I should not have been here this day. I require none with me but this one man,' his friend who waited on him. So set off the melancholy procession, but he with a happy cheerfulness on him.

By the side of the scaffold, a curate said, 'Own our king and we shall pray for you.' He answered, 'I will have none of your prayers; I am come to bear my testimony against you, and such as you are.' The curate persisted, 'Own our king and pray for him, whatever you say against us.' And Renwick replied, 'I will discourse no more with you. I am within a little to appear before Him who is King of kings, and Lord of lords, who shall pour shame, contempt and confusion upon all the kings of the earth who have not ruled for Him.' Calvary, besides being everything else that matters, was an affair of kings, rulers in heaven and in earth over man and in him, and was the complete victory of the King of kings and Lord of lords. How blessed to die in the grace and power of it as died James Renwick!

While the drums beat out their wild disharmony, he magnified and blessed the Lord in singing from the 103rd Psalm, and in reading his last chapter, Revelation 19. Amid all the din, his manly voice thrilled with rapturous faith as he read the words, 'He hath on His vesture and on His thigh a name written, King of kings and Lord of lords.' To prayer he went again while the drums continued their deafening earthborn, earthbound thunder, and was heard of Him in Heaven, His dwelling place.

Humanly, he complained about being disturbed in worship, but assured himself afresh: 'I shall soon be above these clouds; then shall I enjoy Thee and glorify Thee without interruption or intermission forever.' The harsh order was given to him to go up the death ladder. He climbed up and prayed again, being heard to say, 'Lord, I die in the faith that Thou wilt not leave Scotland, but that Thou wilt make the blood of Thy witnesses the seed of Thy church, and return again and be glorious in our land. And now, Lord, I am ready; the Bride the Lamb's wife, hath made herself ready.' The blinding napkin was tied about his face, and he spoke to his friend, close by his side, 'Farewell; be diligent in duty, make your peace with God through Christ. There is a great trial coming. As to the remnant I leave, I have committed them to God. Tell them from me not to weary nor be discouraged in maintaining the testimony, and the Lord will provide you teachers and ministers; and when He comes, He will make these despised truths glorious in the earth.' With his last words in his mouth, 'Lord, into Thy hands I commend my spirit, for Thou hast redeemed me, Lord God of truth,' the hangman turned him over. The Christ-defying drums never ceased their cruel rattling until the death struggles of one of the sweetest martyrs of Jesus were ended. So died the last leader, the beautiful and saintly last leader of the Covenanters, three days beyond his twenty-sixth birthday, joining, as he said, 'my testimony to all that hath been sealed by blood, shed either on scaffolds, fields or seas for the Cause of Christ.' He died for the Crown Rights of the Redeemer against the infamous, impious usurpation of the Stuart kings, of what he, inspired-like, had called 'The Uncommunicable Prerogative of Jehovah,' the Headship of the Kirk of the living God. Helen Alexander, a sufferer in the same cause, reverently wrapped him in his winding sheet, and he was laid away, among the dust of other martyrs in the most despised and neglected corner of Greyfriars Kirkyard, the burial place of criminals, a 'grave with the wicked.'

*

The leaderless, 'bleeding remnant,' through the dark months struggled on living and dying, in their 'sweet believing,' their very enduring their achieving. The last of them known to fall before the Glorious Revolution was George Wood, of Andrew Hislop's age, sixteen or seventeen years, and, like that brave, godly shepherd boy, he lay in the fields. The lines written so feelingly by Dr Veitch of Andrew Hislop will also ever speak of young, fellow-martyr George Wood shot in the night, the night indeed just before the dawn.

> *Coming from the hills that morn,*
> *Doing humble duty well;*
> *Free in step, your honest look*
> *Born of sunlight on the fell.*
>
> *So they left you, martyr brave,*
> *Left you on the reddened sod;*
> *But no raven touched your face;*
> *On it lay the peace of God.*

James Mitchell

James Mitchell

My brother dear, with courage bear the cross,
Joy shall be joined with all thy sorrow here,
High is thy hope, disdain this earthly dross
Soon shall you see the wished-for day appear.
Now it is dark, the sky cannot be clear,
After the clouds it shall be calm anon;
Wait on His will whose blood hath bought thee dear,
Extol His Name, though outward joys be gone.
Look to thy Lord, thou art not left alone,
Since He is thine, what pleasure thou canst take!
He is at hand and hears thy every groan;
End out thy fight, and suffer for His sake.
A sight most bright thy soul shall shortly see,
When store of glory rich reward shall be.

A sonnet written by Lady Culross to John Welsh, prisoner in Blackness Castle.
She wrote a letter also to him and his companions urging them to be thankful
that they were only in the 'darkness of Blackness' and not in the 'blackness of
darkness.' About three months later they were all banished for life.

DURING the afternoon of Saturday, 11 July 1668, a thin
spare man of markedly solemn face, stood at the top of Black-
friars Wynd, near the High Street, Edinburgh. He was a man
who knew that his soul was among lions; a man who lay
among those that were set on fire. He waited for one with
whom day and night in his heart and thoughts, and even in
his prayers, he was at war; one whom he deemed the most
wicked man of his times; one whose tongue was the keenest
sword in all Scotland – James Sharp, Archbishop of St
Andrews.

Ever his eyes turned upon a mansion whose doors must
soon open. What of the homeless, the starving, the disfigured
and maimed? What of the deported, the prisoners and the
martyrs? He himself had suffered too. It was right to do it!

125

James Mitchell

Though many of his fellow-Covenanters said that there were better and more certain weapons than the pistol – faith, hope, love, prayers and tears, yet it was but justice, and that long enough delayed to rid the land of this man-trapping encumbrance. 'One of you is a devil!' He was a Judas indeed! This man who marked the steps of the righteous, waiting for their souls! He must die! James Sharp, Archbishop of St Andrews, and enemy of God, must die! James Mitchell, Covenanter, would kill him!

The stately coach still awaited and the horses hooved the cobblestones; the coachmen looked around dreamily and the man of serious countenance impatiently gripped his silver pistol. He would not carry it much longer now! James Mitchell, *alias* James Small, a James the Less to many, would now accomplish his so great and necessary work!

The mansion doors opened and Archbishop Sharp, Primate of Scotland, came out on to the street. Bishop Honeyman of the Orkney Islands followed him. They moved towards the coach. The Primate got in and sat down. Bishop Honeyman was entering when the Covenanter dashed round to the open side of the vehicle and quickly fired a pistol shot into it. Swiftly he ran across the street to the Niddrie Wynd where he was stopped by a man who let him go on seeing the firearm. Down the Wynd he sped and up the Cowgate, soon reaching Stevenlaw Close and the home of his friend, Fergusson of Caitloch. There, he changed his clothes and went out into the street again where some were saying that a man had been killed in the High Street, but ''Twas only a bishop!'

Though the voice of Walter Mill had long since been silenced in the flames and smoke of his martyr fire, yet his opinion of the king's bishops was still forthrightly that of most people in Scotland. He had said, 'I affirm that they whom you call bishops do not the work of bishops, nor use the office of bishops, but live after their own sensual pleasures, taking no care for the flock nor yet regarding the Word of God.' So, it was only one of such. ' "Twas only a bishop!"

But a bishop had not been killed. One had had a wrist shot through by a pistol bullet. Bishop Honeyman had got what was meant for Archbishop Sharp. James Mitchell whose mind had wilted under persecution pressure was 'Ane ill gunner'; and the spared prelate had got an unforgettable glimpse of 'the lean hollow-cheeked man of truculent countenance.' Years later, someone reported that Sharp 'had a wave of him passing from the coach, and passing the street, which had such impression upon His Grace that the first sight he saw of him after he was taken he knew him to be the person who shot the shot.'

James Mitchell, Covenanter! Who was he? What was his life? He was born and nurtured in times of suffering for the godly, had a saving conversion to Christ and a call to His ministry; was a poor but earnest student at Edinburgh University where he graduated with a Master of Arts degree, and where he also signed the National Covenant, and the Solemn League and Covenant, both tendered to him by Robert Leighton, later Archbishop Leighton of Glasgow, who kept them not himself. But private tutor and chaplain, James Mitchell of undeceived heart, kept them in life and in death. There was not much chance in his times for one of his principles – 'That good youth that had not much to subsist upon, and fit for a school, or the teaching of gentlemen's children.'

After the sorrowful field of Rullion Green, 1666, where tragically died many Bible-loving and prayerful men along with the two godly ministers from Northern Ireland, Andrew McCormick and John Crookshanks, Mitchell had joined the shuttle service between Scotland and Holland whereby men went to the flat lands for safety; men whose love for the grand old Cause would not let them stay there long. Within the year he had returned. Now was a time he might have gone again, but he did not; now when there was a great price on his head, and a very revengeful ecclesiastic longing for appeasement, and offers of pardons for any tell-tale accomplices, of whom years later Mitchell avowed that he had none, and in all his sufferings bravely mentioned no name in his crime but his own. Now was a time he might have gone, but nobly he stayed. For the next six years he fended for himself as best he could, and eventually with his wife opened a little shop in Edinburgh.

The 1666 Rising in the West Country with its tragic climax at Rullion Green within sight of Edinburgh, gave the rulers coward excuse for an aftermath orgy of fines, imprisonments, banishments, tortures and death sentences. Their corrupt selves corrupted all, and they who spoke of peace knew not the meaning of it. Only among the mountains was there peace, and righteousness among the little hills. There they who knew the power of evil men could still sing,

> *In God I trust; I will not fear*
> *What man can do to me.*
> *Thy vows upon me are, O God,*
> *I'll render praise to Thee.*

They had to sing very softly, all the same; for, at the crack of James Mitchell's pistol shot, persecuting zeal threw itself more fiercely into the saddle. There were those who could fire a hundred shots for his one, and aim more surely too. They were now looking for targets. Galloping squadrons beat the moors for human game. Those who had suffered before suffered again. Cropped ears were better hidden. Anyone who possibly had any fellow-feeling with the bad marksman were painfully cross-examined. Godly women, such as the widows, Margaret Kello and Ann Duncan, the latter with her children beside her, lay in jail for months, were heavily fined and banished to the plantations. Ann Duncan was saved from torture by the lone voice of the Earl of Rothes. Huge fines were imposed, and churches had neither ministers nor worshippers. Sharp, the man to whom God had been so merciful, was called to London by the king, and was asked by him to put into practice a policy of moderation, toleration, and indulgence, a policy of let us all be neither hot nor cold and eventually freeze together in religious frills – with, of course, the utter stamping out of these boorish conventicles! These meetings where people would persist in reading the Bible for themselves, and where one's speech was judged as to whether what one said was Scriptural or not! where title, pedigree, art and ceremony meant nothing! One attended these conventicles as one who knew the grace of God in Christ Jesus, or as one who did not. There, Covenanters renewed fellowship with God and with one another so helping to prevent their following afar off when they might be caught unawares and deny their Saviour.

Through a welter of anger and anguish, laws, lawyers and liars, the outlawed Covenanters were out, Christ-companioned in the wilderness, and were certainly not as reeds shaken in the winds; while their enemies lived delicately wicked in kings' houses. The years 1668 to 1674 passed into history with some souls making sure by their sufferings that they would reign with Him. There was no union, nor could there be, with those who made their king their god and those whose God was King.

James Mitchell

Early in 1674 plain-spoken Robert Douglas died. He had been the celebrant at the Scots Coronation of Charles II, and was a staunch Presbyterian and Covenanter. He referred to the proposed church government of Archbishop Sharp as 'a stinking weed that the Lord will root up.' A kindly Scot, he was a Douglas worthy of the name. He died, and Sharp was at his funeral. Among the mourners there he saw a sombre face that he thought he had seen before. A few days later, while passing down a street, he saw it again. The earnest eyes of it gazed intently at him. The thin man standing in the shop doorway was the man who had fired the unforgettable, unforgivable shot! With all speed but under pretence of another errand, he sent Sir William Sharp, his brother, with armed helpers to take the Covenanter shopkeeper. Wrote Mitchell later from the Tolbooth, 'He took me under the pretence of having spoken with me on other matters, I not knowing him until five or six of his servants were laying fast hold on me. They being armed of purpose, desired that I would excuse him, seeing what he had done was upon his brother's account; which excuse I easily admitted, seeing that he thought himself obliged to do what he did to me without law or order, in the behalf of his brother. Much more was I obliged to do what I did in the behalf of many brethren whose oppression was so great, and whose blood he caused to be shed in such abundance.'

Quickly Mitchell was rushed before the Commissioner and Privy Council. Perjurers three, My Lords Rothes, Hatton and Primrose, were selected to question him. Sharp sent Nicol Somerville, brother-in-law of the prisoner, to tell him that his life would be spared if he would confess his crime. Mitchell said that he was quite willing to do so, if he could have assurance of this in the name of the king. This was given. In the Minutes of the Privy Council is this record, 'He then did confess upon his knees he was the person upon assurance given him by one of the Committy as to his life, who had warrand from the Lord Commissioner and Council to give the same.' Two days later he was again questioned and repeated his confession. Vindictively he was condemned to have his right hand cut off at the Cross of Edinburgh, and to 'forfeit his whole goods and posterity.' The king was to be told about it first! He was then handed on to the Justiciary Court which met on 2 March 1674. Before it began, one of the judges who was no friend of the Primate, knowing the wicked designs that were set upon the Covenanter, whispered to him in passing, 'Confess nothing unless you are sure of your limbs as well as of your life.' This made Mitchell very wary, and he took up another quite legal position; he would confess nothing, and retracted what he had said! His judges were at a loss. Courts met again on 12 and 25 March, but nothing could be made of the charge. The Lord Advocate deserted it, and James Mitchell, who should have been set at liberty, was unlawfully taken back to prison.

There were Covenanters who escaped from the Canongate Tolbooth. James Mitchell was one of those who tried to do so but failed, and his unsuccessful bid for freedom, in 1675, gave his captors the further chance to do some legal brutalizing on him. A blended inquisition of judges and nobles tried him during the evening of 18 January 1676. Their aim was to convict him of being in the Rising of 1666, and of being the assassin of 1668. They were prepared to go to all lengths for a confession of his crimes. Mitchell knew what he was facing, and, being a man of very astute mind, he held them off, saying, 'I humbly conceive that both by the law of the nation and the practice of the house at that time, I ought

131

James Mitchell

to have been set at liberty; yet notwithstanding, I was, contrary both to law, justice and equity, returned to prison.' Judicially, he would admit nothing. His judges panicked, and the weak nobleman in the chair, Lord Linlithgow, said, 'Sir, we will make you confess.'

Four days later, the Covenanter again stood before them. Grim machines of torture, the Boot, mallet and wedges, lay on the table, but Mitchell would acknowledge nothing. The noble chairman, pointing to the Boot, said, 'I will see if that will make you confess.' The Covenanter was at his best when the odds were at their greatest against him, and James Mitchell at once took up the challenge. 'My Lord,' he said, 'I confess that by torture you may cause me to blaspheme God, as Saul compelled the saints; you may cause me to speak amiss of your Lordships; to call myself a thief or a murderer, and then panel me on it; but, if you shall have me put to it, I profess before God and your Lordships, that nothing extorted from me by torture shall be made use of against me in judgment, nor have any force in law against me or any other person.' They said that he had the logic of the devil. Said Mitchell drily, 'I acknowledge no such thing.' They were routed and annoyed.

Two days afterwards, on the 24 March 1674, in the Inner Parliament House, Protestant Scotland had sitting a full-robed court, bearing an iniquitous likeness to one from the Spanish Inquisition. A lone prisoner marked with suffering stood in the midst of it. He knew well enough that the more he confessed, the greater would be the torture exacted upon him to make him confess still more. Present were the Boot and the executioner. The judges haggled and cajoled, but Covenanter Mitchell stood firm. They wilted and sentenced him to torture. He boldly testified to them and told them that when they pleased they could call forward the executioner. This they did.

Coming forward, the executioner tied Mitchell in a chair. The Boot was brought, and he asked the judges which leg had to be taken. They told him to take either, and he took Mitchell's left leg, and put it into the Boot. The Covenanter took it out again saying, 'Since the judges have not determined, take the better of the two; for I freely bestow it in the Cause,' and he placed his right leg in the cruel instrument of torture. Lord Advocate Nisbet then pompously got up and asked leave from the Chairman to say a word or two. He went on at great length on the function and power of the magistrate. It was an attempt to justify their cruelty. The Covenanter, his right leg still lying in the Boot, and he tied to the chair, entered into a debate with him. Nisbet came out of it with his crest drooping.

The order was given for the torture to begin. Mitchell said 'My Lords, not knowing that I shall escape this torture with my life, therefore, I beseech you to remember what Solomon saith, 'He who showeth no mercy shall have judgment without mercy.'' And now, my Lords, I do freely from my heart forgive you who are sitting judges upon the bench, and the men who are appointed to be about this horrible piece of work.' As far as his sins were concerned, he added, his trust was in Christ for the full forgiveness of them all.

During this time, the Boot with Mitchell's leg in it had been set on a chest. The hangman took it down and put it on the floor. Upwards of thirty questions were asked of Mitchell in his excruciating torture. Nine times the wedges were driven in with the same question always at every stroke, 'Anything more to say?' The reply, too, was always the same, 'No,

James Mitchell

my lords.' It faded in power as the torture proceeded. On the eighth stroke, the lips moved in a poignantly discernible and resolute, 'No, my lords', and, on the ninth, the Covenanter swooned away. The hangman cried out, 'He is gone, my lords. He is gone!' The judges ordered him to stop. The stately lords then got up and walked out. James Mitchell, Covenanter, had won.

After he was released from the Boot and had recovered a little, with a leg sickening to see, and on which he now could no longer walk, he was carried back by friends, in his torture chair, to the prison. Further tortures were determined upon him; but, it is said, Sharp got news that, in that case, someone would aim more certainly than Mitchell did. The tortured and crushed Covenanter was left to lie painfully in his cell.

Maimed James Mitchell remained for about another year in the dungeons of the Tolbooth, and, in January 1677, with the shining saint James Frazer of Brea, he was taken to the squalid prison on the Bass Rock in the Firth of Forth. Dunnottar Castle, Blackness Castle and the Bass! All are sea-girt Covenanter prisons where Christ and men kept tryst! 'A melancholy place,' Frazer called the Bass. While there, he testified that he thought he found in himself some increase 'in gifts, knowledge and grace; some further discoveries of the knowledge of Christ and the Gospel I never had before.' Life there was hard. Sustenance sometimes was 'snow water or corrupted water sprinkled over with a little oatmeal to drink, and some dried fish.' James Frazer had no smashed limbs. He could go at times to 'a garden where herbs grow, with some cherry trees, of the fruit of which I several times tasted.' Mitchell lay in the darkness of the prison, the Lord a light about him preparing him for the blaze of His glory. He who had borne the image of the earthly was getting ready to bear the image of the heavenly. Fellowship among those on the Bass was precious. What must it have been among such men as Peden, Hog, Blackadder, Frazer and Mitchell? Says Frazer, 'Sometimes, when they would take it in their heads, they would shut us all close up, and not suffer any of us to speak to another.' That was affliction. 'But,' says Frazer, 'our patience overcame it.' It is a revealing book, *The Book of the Intricacies of My Heart*, and a wonderful record of the free grace of God in Christ Jesus.

In about another year, lame and dungeon-marked James Mitchell was taken from the Bass. Sharp did not want him to live even there. Noblemen who could have saved him from the jaws of the lion did not interfere. Their fears one of another had them all ensnared. Rothes, Hatton, Lauderdale, and Sir William Sharp could not or would not speak the truth. Nicol Somerville alone stood firm on the promise given by the lords and judges to James Mitchell on his first confession. The Covenanter himself produced a copy of the Act of the Council issued against him on 12 March 1674, in which the promise of life upon confession was recognized. He asked for the original to be shown. This request was over-ruled as out of order on the grounds of informality. His last trials were shameful. Any guilt that could be attached to him was 'lost in the complicated perfidy, cruelty, perjury and revenge which accomplished his death.'

On Thursday 10 January 1678, his sentence was pronounced, 'That Mr James Mitchell be taken to the Grassmarket of Edinburgh upon Friday, the 18th January instant, betwixt two and four of the clock in the afternoon, and there hanged on a gibbet till he be dead, and all his moveables, goods and gear, escheat, and inbrought to his majesty's use.' This court had no sooner broken up than the lords found the act recorded that Mitchell had appealed for. It was signed by Lord Rothes. 'This action,' says Bishop Burnet, 'and all concerned in it, were looked on by the people with horror; and it was such a complication of treachery, perjury and cruelty, as the like had perhaps not been known.' Not content with the unjust sentence passed, two days later the court said that they wanted James Mitchell's head and hands to be exposed in some prominent public place in the city. This request was turned down on the grounds that nothing more could be added to the sentence.

Elizabeth Somerville, the wife of James Mitchell, not many days before delivered of a child, wrote a letter to the Lords of the Privy Council expressing 'an ardent desire to see her husband, and to take her long farewell of him before he die,' this being 'her only worldly desire,' and would they 'for the love of Christ be graciously pleased to reprieve the foresaid sentence for such a time.' No attention was given to her request.

The letter addressed to Mitchell from Rotterdam by 'Your Brother in the Lord, J.C.J.B.,' must have been refreshing to him. 'I would not fail to let you know, that we were much refreshed to hear how the Lord helped you to be faithful in that sharp piece of trial,' writes the man whose name is only letters; and he urges, 'Stand fast in His truth in His strength, and as hitherto He has not deserted any that were willing to witness a good confession and cause, so may you through grace expect by faith the same supply of assistance and through-bearing grace. And if herein you be helped you are blessed that ever you had a life to quit for that cause and interest, and being lent you, to give it back on so noble terms.'

In the few days left to him, James Mitchell got together what are now known as 'The Papers Left by James Mitchell.' 'Me, who may justly call myself less than the least of all saints, and the chiefest of all sinners, yet Christ Jesus calleth to be a witness for his despised truth, and trampled-on interests and cause.' He prepared, too, his speech for the scaffold in which he says: 'I am brought unjustly to this place, but I acknowledge that my particular and private sins have been such as have merited a worse death unto me. But I die in the hope of the merits of Jesus Christ to be freed from the eternal punishment due to me for sin.' And 'I wish heartily that this my poor life may put an end to the persecution of the true members of Christ in this kingdom.' And 'In testimony to the cause of Christ, I at this time willingly lay down my life.' He was to try hard to read this speech from the scaffold but could not for the beating of the drums, and he threw it over the side of the platform.

Had James Sharp been merciful to James Mitchell he would have been most merciful to himself; but the afternoon of 18 January came with him gathering ecclesiastically and unmercifully his cruel desserts around him. Shadows of death on Magus Muir were taking living shape. 'Judgment without mercy!' It was on the faces of the sad silent men in the crowds; and the vast crowds of sympathizing tearful women might have made Sharp think of the Scripture, 'Blessed are the merciful: for they shall obtain mercy.'

The people filled the streets. Special guards were put on in great strength. It was rumoured that an attempt at his rescue would be made by women; and, says the scurrilous and sarcastic author of *Ravillac Redivivus*, 'There was never seen such an appearance of that sex at any execution, as was at his, where a body of at least seven hundred sisters stood together almost in rank and file.' No doubt many of them had heavy hearts for a sick wife, and the new-born baby that Mitchell had never seen. James Mitchell was greatly loved, and he drew comfort from it that day. In the eight days between his sentence and his death, he received big sums of money in private gifts, 'which,' says cynical *Ravillac Redivivus*, 'was interpreted by the party for the particular care that God had of him, who never sees the righteous forsaken nor their seed begging their bread.'

The Covenanter the night before his death had asked the Provost of the city for room around the scaffold for the large number of his friends who were going to attend in mourning. This was refused. For this *Ravillac* deemed the Provost 'honest and prudent.'

James Mitchell had heard that he would not be allowed to speak. He had written out two copies of his last speech and hidden them in his Psalm Book. Taking one copy out, he began to read it; but Babel and Bedlam were great allies of his adversaries, and the noise of the drums was so great, he gave up reading in despair, and the papers fluttered over the scaffold to be picked up by ready and careful hands. Next day, copies of this speech were posted up as a testimony in various places in the city. He asked for a Psalm to be sung, he joining in with his friends. He then climbed the ladder, with voice and life saying, 'Amen and Amen.'

Says *Ravillac Redivivus*, 'After his Body was cut down, it was conveyed to Magdalen Chapel, from whence it was carried to burial in great pomp, being attended by at least forty mourners, whereof the Justice General's Gentleman was one. It is reported that the hearse cloth was of velvet, but certain it is, it was more than ordinary brave.'

He won a place in Patrick Walker's shining lists, 'Our McKails, Welwoods, Mitchells, Kings, Kidds, Blackadders, Camerons, Cargills, Pedens, Renwicks, Shields, with all the rest of the faithful followers of the Lamb; and if it might be supposed that they could be diverted from thinking and speaking of His decease which he did accomplish at Jerusalem, and from what they have felt, seen and heard since they left us, they would stand astonished, and not own us for their successors, that have come so far short of their piety, zeal and faithfulness, and few or none walking in the pathed way that they chalked out for us: and few or none contending earnestly for substance and circumstances, hair and hoof of that dear-bought testimony, that they handed down to us by their fightings, wrestlings, prayers, tears, and blood, for the which they counted nothing too dear, and now let so easily slip through our slippery, feeble, feel-less fingers. What's easily come by is oft easily parted with.'

Then what of us, and our day?

William Gordon

William Gordon

Call to Judah in her blindness;
Bid benighted Israel hear;
Drop the word of truth and kindness
On the heathen's palsied ear!
Trim thy lamp — the night hours cheering;
Wash thy robes from every stain;
Watch to hail the glad appearing
Of the Bridegroom and His train!
Haste, thy coming Lord to greet!
Cast thy crown before His feet!
Only, may His quest for thee
Find thee what He made thee — free.

HARRIET S. MENTEITH, Lays of the Kirk and Covenant

MOST of the three hundred and sixty-five letters of the banished Covenanter, Samuel Rutherford — 'A man,' as he once said of himself, 'often borne down and hungry, and waiting for the Marriage Supper of the Lamb' — were first published in Holland in 1664. They were edited by an exiled Covenanter, 'The Great MacWard.' Three years previously Rutherford had died, calling for a well-tuned harp, and witnessing that 'Glory, Glory dwelleth in Immanuel's Land.' 'A land that has more than four summers in the year!' he wrote. 'What a singing life is there! There is not a dumb bird in all that large field, but all sing and breathe out heaven, joy, glory, and dominion to the High Prince of that new-found land; and, verily, the land is sweeter that He is the glory of that land . . . O how sweet to be wholly Christ's, and wholly

143

in Christ; to dwell in Immanuel's high and blessed land, and live in that sweetest air where no wind bloweth but the breathings of the Holy Ghost, no sea nor floods flow but the pure Water of Life that floweth from and under the Throne and from the Lamb; no planting but the Tree of Life that yieldeth twelve manner of fruits every month! What do we here but sin and suffer! O when shall the night be gone, the shadows flee away, and the morning of the long, long day without cloud or night dawn! The Spirit and the Bride say, Come! ... O when shall the Lamb's wife be ready, and the Bridegroom say, Come!'

While men were demanding that he attend upon their unjust courts that they might sentence him to hang upon the gallows, and he was being troubled that because of illness he could not be there to receive such a sentence, his Master called him away to enjoy himself forever among the things that He has prepared for them who love Him.

Three hundred and sixty-five letters! One a day to read for a year! Never voice spoke out of a heart more abundantly filled with the love of Christ. These letters are the revealed soul of a man who fell asleep at night talking of Christ; who spoke of Him during his sleep, and whose dreams were of Christ. These are the letters of a man who confessed, 'I have not been so faithful in the end as I was in the beginning of my ministry, when sleep departed from mine eyes through care for Christ's lambs'; and of a man who wrote to Gordon of Cardoness, 'Thoughts of your soul depart not from me in my sleep.'

The name of Gordon is honoured in these letters. If we include those written to Lady Kenmure, who was a Gordon by her first marriage, it means that nearly a hundred of them were written to people of that name. There are letters to Gordons of Cardoness, Knockbreck, Roberton, Knockgray, White-park, Rusco, Ayr, Garloch, and Earlston. 'Pull at your soul, and draw it aside from the company it is with,' he urges them, 'and whisper into it news of eternity, death, judgment, heaven and hell . . . Consider the necessity of salvation and tell me in the ear of God if ye have made it sure.' The lists of the sufferers show how well they and their families did so; and how greatly they truly merited his correspondence! In shining succession come the names: 'Alexander Gordon, sentenced to death; Edward Gordon, hanged without trial; John Gordon, of Largmore, died of wounds received at Pentland; John Gordon, shot without trial; John Gordon of Irongray, executed for being present at Pentland; John and Robert Gordon, his brother, of Knockbreck, executed for being present at Pentland; Nathaniel Gordon, executed at St Andrews.' And so on, the faithful unto death, crowned with life!

Writing about John and Robert Gordon of Knockbrex and their people, Wodrow says, 'The two young gentlemen at this time executed, I have it from persons yet alive of their acquaintance that they were youths of shining piety and good learning and parts. The harassings and losses of the family cannot be estimated, they were so frequent and severe.' Hanged with other eight Covenanters, the Knockbreck Gordons died clasped in each other's arms. Those ten were the ready first-fruits of the prisoners from Rullion Green. Besides leaving written individual testimonies, of which some appear to be lost, the ten wrote also a joint testimony, and in it say, 'As we were not afraid to take our lives in our hands, so we are not afraid to lay them down in this cause; and as we are not ashamed of Christ because of His cross, so we would not have you offended because of us; for we bear you record that we would not exchange lots with our adversaries, nor redeem our lives, liberties and fortunes, at the price of perjury, and breach of covenant.' And again, 'Though our eyes shall not see it, yet we believe that the Sun of Righteousness shall arise with healing in His wings; and that He will repair the breaches, build the old wastes, and raise up the desolations.' One by one, on the day they died, they signed it with the hands that soon were to be cut off, and put up in Lanark, for there they had uplifted them to God when taking the Covenant. Some of them signed also another testimony along with Thomas Paterson, who died of his wounds before he could be sentenced. They were in the same cell with him. 'O what a sweet couple, what a glorious yoke are youth and grace, Christ and a young man,' says Samuel Rutherford.

> *Gang, hert, untae the Lamp o Licht;*
> *Gang, hert, dae service an honour;*
> *Gang, hert, an serve Him day an nicht;*
> *Gang, hert, untae thy Saviour.*

William Gordon of Earlston was a member of a family whose spiritual history had its beginnings in the death of Patrick Hamilton, the twenty-four-year-old converted-to-Christ noble and priest, and noble protomartyr of the Scottish Reformation. It is said that the Alexander Gordon of that eventful day, though still a youth, was compelled to sign the sentence that doomed that great young man to the stake; but the convincing Scriptural arguments and the steadfast faith of Hamilton shook him greatly, and he set himself earnestly to know the truth. In the mercy of God, a Wycliffe New Testament came his way. This he read in secluded and little-known parts of the Woods of Airds near his home. Believing the Word himself, he gathered others around him to listen to his readings, and the Gospel began to spread over a great deal of

Galloway. He obtained a godly English Lollard as tutor for his eldest son, and the grace of God began and continued in the family. Alexander Gordon died at a ripe old age, a man of deeply spiritual experience.

The record of the Gordons of Earlston from that early day of the Reformed Faith till the times of the Covenanters was one of constancy and piety. They were Christians and Protestants *par excellence*.

Alexander Gordon, the father of William, took his place nobly in the Earlston line of valorous grace. He was a friend of Samuel Rutherford, and there are extant eight letters to him, and one to Lady Earlston, his wife, from 'The little fair man.'

The first letter was evidently written in Rutherford's house at Anwoth, 'The Buss o' Bield,' or 'The Bush of Shelter.' In it he refers to Alexander Gordon as the first man in Galloway to be called out and questioned for the Name of Jesus, and says, 'Christ hath said, "Alexander Gordon shall lead the ring in witnessing a good confession," and therefore He hath put the garland of suffering for Himself first upon your head . . . Sir, ye were never honourable until now.' The second letter is a short one, written in Edinburgh when the Pastor of Anwoth had been taken from his flock and was now on his way into banishment. It is signed, 'In haste making for my palace at Aberdeen,' which palace was a prison. The witness of that letter is resplendent. 'No king is better provided for than I am,' he writes. 'Sweet, sweet and easy is the cross of my Lord. My chains are over-gilded with gold. No pen, no words, no genius, can express to you the loveliness of my only Lord Jesus.'

Other five to Alexander Gordon, Earlston the Elder, and the one to Lady Earlston, his wife, were written in Aberdeen, now an Isle of Patmos to 'Christ's prisoner.' Rutherford

William Gordon

seemed apprehensive of her spiritual condition and advised her, 'Make an end of your accounts with your Lord; for death and judgment are tides that bide no man.' For himself he rejoiced, saying, 'My Lord hath made me well content of a borrowed fireside and a borrowed bed. I am feasted with the joys of the Holy Ghost. I would I had help to praise Him.'

The last letter of the correspondence was written in London. The letters written from Earlston we can never know – the letters that Samuel Rutherford longed for and was so glad to receive. It is a small enough remnant of a correspondence that went on for at least ten years. Nine letters! It is a small remnant but a blessed and a treasured one. In those years, Earlston the Elder led the ring in Galloway and was harassed and harried, tried and spoiled. Without grace it was utterly unbearable; but, amid the sufferings, fines and hard sentences until the end, Alexander Gordon, for the Name of Jesus led the ring. Towards the close, 'His grace-proud pastor' in the great city of London wrote to the afflicted saint among the hills of Galloway, 'And, if ye be near the water side, as I know ye are, all that I can say is this, Sir, that I feel by the smell of that land which is before you that it is a goodly country, and it is well paid for to your hand. And He is before you who will heartily welcome you.'

John Livingstone, in his *Characteristics*, says of Alexander Gordon, 'He was a man of great spirit but much subdued by inward exercise. For wisdom, courage, and righteousness he might have been a magistrate in any part of the earth.'

William Gordon, Earlston the Younger, was acquainted early in life with suffering for Christ. He saw his parents continuously through the years pay a big price for serving the Lord. He had sometimes to flee and watch the pillaging of Earlston House. His safe vantage point was sometimes a bushy corner of the Woods of Airds, or a leafy branch of the big oak tree near Earlston House gates. In winter he had to run faster and go farther. 'Remember me to your eldest son,' wrote Rutherford to Alexander Gordon – this same son, William, who even in his youth had much of his father's generous spirit and holy ways upon him. 'He was,' says John Howie of Lochgoin, 'a gentleman of high and honourable attainments devoted to religion and godliness.'

He came of age in persecution for righteousness' sake when some King's Council Commissioners wrote a letter to him, well knowing what his reply would be, concerning the settling of an unwanted non-Covenanting minister in a vacant parish. They said in it, 'Finding the church of Dalry to be one of those to which the bishop hath presented an actual minister, Mr George Henry, fit and qualified for the charge, and that the gentleman is to come to your parish this Sabbath next, to preach to that people, and that you are a person of special interest there, we do require you to cause this edict to be served, and the congregation to convene and countenance him, so as to be encouraged to prosecute his ministry in that place.' Names were signed with a great flourish at the bottom of it. The writers well knew William Gordon's principles, and what he was like in all matters of conscience. They knew that he would refuse what they wanted; they then would have a charge against him.

William Gordon wrote a reply the very next day, 22 May 1663. He said, 'I ever judged it safest to obey God, and stand at a distance from whatsoever doth not tend to God's glory, and the edification of the souls of His scattered people, of which that congregation is a part . . . I have already determined therein, with the consent of the people, to a truly worthy and qualified person, that he may be admitted to exercise his gift among that people; and for me to countenance the bearer of your Lordship's letter, were most impiously and dishonourably to wrong the Majesty of God, and violently to take away the Christian liberty of His afflicted people, and enervate my own right.' They had got their desire! On 30 July, they wrote ordering him to appear before them 'to answer for his seditions and factious carriage.' This is what they called his being true to his conscience and the persecuted people of God. He bore their judgment, but continued as before.

On 24 November of that same year, they wrote to him: 'The Council being informed that the Laird of Earlston kept conventicles and private meetings in his house, do order letters to be directed against him, to appear in court before this Council, to answer for his contempt, under pain of rebellion.' Dauntlessly he kept his godly way. The Gospel was persecuted. Why not he? In the Woods of Airds and Corsack very gracious meetings were being held. Displaced ministers were eagerly listened to there by large crowds, and William Gordon sponsored their presence. The Council again wrote to him. This time they said that he had attended these meetings in the Woods of Airds. He had listened to Gabriel Semple, a Covenanter minister, in these woods; he had heard the Scriptures expounded by rebels both in his mother's house and in his own, and he was 'to abstain from all such meetings in time coming, and to live peaceably and orderly, and conform to law.' He chose to obey God rather than man, and the Council sentenced him to banishment. He was to depart from Britain within a month, and never to return again or he would be hanged. During his last days, the month at home, he was to live peaceably, or he would be fined £10,000, or sent to prison.

It appears that Earlston paid no heed to their threats at all. The righteous man held on his way. The persecutors piled hardships upon him, insidious, vindictive and devilish; and, in the year 1667, they turned him and his family out of Earlston House altogether. The home of his fathers became the barracks of dragoon garrisons; the plunderers sheltered in the home of the plundered.

Earlston House was occupied by Sir William Bannatyne, and he sent out marauding parties up and down Galloway. Wodrow says, 'They exercised inexpressible cruelties upon any they were pleased to allege had been at Pentland, or conversed with such. One, David McGill, in that parish, whom they came to apprehend, escaped happily from them in women's clothes, but dreadful was the way taken with his poor wife whom they alleged accessory to her husband's escape. They seized her and bound her, and put lighted matches between her fingers for several hours: the torture and the pain made her almost distracted. She lost one of her hands, and in a few days she died. They pillaged the country round about as they pleased . . . Bannatyne in this country never refused to let his men rob and plunder wherever they pleased. His oppressions, murders, robberies, rapes, adulteries, and so on, were so many and atrocious that the managers themselves were ashamed of them.' Bannatyne eventually had to fly abroad, and died in abject misery.

The last twelve years of the life of William Gordon had many trials and punishments, studied and unmerciful. But for grace upon grace through which his faith came out of his fiery trials more precious than gold, he would have failed under their malevolent and vexatious power.

The year 1679 saw many a tried Covenanter laid away to rest. Amongst them was Earlston the Younger, William Gor-

William Gordon

don. A member of the worshipping Kirk 'ahint the dyke,' the praying Kirk of God, when it gathered together at Bothwell to uphold its banner 'The Lord our Righteousness,' he, too, would be there, if he could. It was a long way from Earlston to Bothwell, and it seems that he thought that Heaven might be at the end of it. He sent on his son Alexander before him, and went off to settle his business affairs. He then hurried on to join 'The Remnant.'

'The strife was o'er, the battle won' for many of the defeated Covenanters before he came near Bothwell. Sufferers were fleeing before the pursuing dragoons and he did not even know of the disaster when a party of the King's Cavalry surrounded him. They called upon him to surrender, and yield to their demands. He would not do so, and there fought his last fight, dying where he stood. His body was thrown into a ditch, and lay there several days until friends interred it secretly in Glassford Churchyard. His Bible and sword are still preserved.

His son, Alexander, had a marvellous escape from capture. He was sent to Holland to represent the Covenanter United Societies. Coming home, he was taken prisoner, put to the torture, and sent to the prisons of the Bass and Blackness until the Glorious Revolution of 1688 when he was liberated.

Of letters written by Samuel Rutherford to William Gordon there are only four in the immortal collection. They were all written when Gordon was quite a young man, and all were written in the one year, 1637. What a spiritual young man Earlston the Younger must have been to have such letters written to him. All are from Aberdeen. Deep calls unto deep in them. William Gordon could evidently write letters refreshing to the soul of Rutherford. Says Rutherford in his first one to the youth, 'The devil can cause Christ's glooms [frowns] to speak a lie to a weak man.' Sometimes, no doubt, in the stern years of Earlston he wrestled over that. But we know that he also did what his great pastor advised, 'Now, Sir, in your youth gather fast; your sun will mount to the meridian quickly, and thereafter decline. Be greedy of grace. Study above anything, my dear brother, to mortify your lusts. Oh, but pride of youth, vanity, lusts, idolising of the world, and charming pleasures, take long time to root out ... When the day of visitation comes, and your old idols come weeping about you, ye will have much ado not to break your heart. It is best to give up in time with them, so as ye could at a call quit your part of this world for a drink of water, or a thing of nothing.' William Gordon had not many letters of Samuel Rutherford's but he had this one, and at least the other three, all his very own.

The second letter is a long one. It is evident that young William Gordon had written about his temptations and his passions that might carry him away like a flood, bringing sin and death. It is a letter for Christian young men, and indeed all Christian men. How can such a letter be quoted from? How it thrills and fills, prays, preaches, praises, goes down to hell, and mounts up to heaven to gather around the redeemed soul and the Lamb that was slain. Samuel Rutherford! Carried up into the third heaven by way of the Cross, seeing things unlawful to be uttered, but all summed up in 'Worthy is the Lamb that was slain!' William Gordon was in need. But, says Rutherford, 'He that can tell his tale, and send such a letter to Heaven as he hath sent to Aberdeen, it is very like he will come speed with Christ.' And he advises Earlston, 'At our first conversion, our Lord putteth the meat in young bairns' mouths with His own hand; but when we grow to some further perfection, we must take Heaven by violence, and take by violence from Christ what we get.' There is no doubt that the young Covenanter proved this so.

The third letter relates how Samuel Rutherford longs to hear from his young friend, and there is praise for the infinite wisdom that has carved out the way of the Cross; and Rutherford's testimony is, 'I rejoice in the hope of that glory to be revealed, for it is no uncertain glory that we look for. Our hope is not hung upon such an untwisted thread as, "I imagine so," or "It is likely," but the cable, the strong tow of our fastened anchor, is the oath and promise of Him who is eternal verity. Our salvation is fastened with God's own hand, and with Christ's own strength, to the strong stake of God's unchangeable nature.'

In the fourth and last known letter between the two, the song rises between Aberdeen and Earlston mounting to the Throne. 'Christ triumphs in me, blessed be His Name. I have all things. I burden no man. I see that this earth and the fulness thereof is my Father's. Sweet, sweet is the Cross of my Lord. The blessing of God upon the Cross of my Lord Jesus! My enemies have contributed, beside their design, to make me blessed. This is my palace, not my prison . . . I think this is all, to gain Christ. All other things are shadows, dreams, fancies, and nothing.' With all his heart William Gordon said 'Amen': with all he was and all he had until he fell, noble soul, on the Bothwell Road. Both say now as they said to each other in their correspondence, ever thinking of Him, 'Praised be the Winner.'

John Dick

John Dick

Come, stingless Death, have o'er! Lo! here's my pass,
In blood charactered by His hand who was,
And is, and shall be. Jordan, cut thy stream –
Make channels dry! I bear my Father's name
Stamped on my brow. I'm ravished with my crown,
I shine so bright. Down with all glory – down –
That world can give. I see the peerless port,
The golden street, the blessed soul's resort,
The tree of life – floods, gushing from the throne,
Call me to joys. Begone, short woes, begone!
I live to die – but now I die to live –
I now enjoy more than I could believe.
The promise me unto possession sends.
Faith in fruition; hope in vision ends.

A Sonnet by John McClelland, Covenanter,
written a few hours before he died

JOHN DICK was a son of David Dick, solicitor in Edinburgh. He was a graduate of Edinburgh University and studied theology there in high hope of becoming a minister of the Gospel among his fellow-Covenanters; but, in the severe orderings of his day, he gained the martyr crown before he could be set apart by his brethren for that great work. He did so well what James Welwood did himself, and advised all such sufferers to do: 'Put on courage in these sad times; brave times for the chosen soldiers of Jesus Christ to show their courage into; brave times, offering brave opportunities for showing forth the braveness of spirit in suffering; that love, that loyalty, that meekness, that patience, and every Christian virtue, that cannot be shown forth in not suffering times.' Over his short life can thus readily be written, 'Are they ministers of Christ? so am I.'

John Dick

Lord Fountainhall scornfully called him 'A Cargillian.'
The compilers of *The Cloud of Witnesses* named him, 'That
worthy gentleman, Mr. John Dick, student of theology.'
Wodrow, the historian, referred to him as, 'This pious and
zealous sufferer'; and Patrick Walker's word for him was,
'That singular Christian and cheerful sufferer, Mr John Dick.'
After his death, when his 'Testimony to the Doctrine, Worship, Discipline and Government of the Church of Scotland
as it was Professed in the Three Kingdoms,' was published,
his friends who brought it out said that he was 'That truly
pious, eminently faithful, and now glorified martyr, Mr John
Dick.'

Though not present at Drumclog, on 20 June 1679, when
Claverhouse dropped his colours and fled from the field, while
John King, up till then his prisoner, laughingly called after
him to stay and hear afternoon sermon, John Dick heartily
joined in the joyful encouragement of it all. It was a gleam of
gladsome sunshine in a dark and cloudy day; and so soon the
Covenanters were to be engulfed unmercifully in the fierce
storm of Bothwell Brig. Dick, the student of theology, wrote
later of 'the pitiful thing,' on his badly-wounded charger
dashing from Drumclog, 'where there fell on either side pret-
tier men than himself.' That day, eighteen-year-old soldier,
linguist, mathematician and poet, William Cleland, gripped
fast the bridle of 'the sorry charger,' of 'the small and fearsome
man,' and would have taken him had he had instant help.
Thinking of this incident, John Dick referred to 'the blood-
thirsty wretch Claverhouse,' who yet must stand before God
on the Judgment Day, and asked, 'Is it possible that the pitiful
thing can think to secure himself by the fleetness of his horse?'
Claverhouse, it is evident from his letters, regretted more the
loss of his animal through wounds at Drumclog, than he did

his men who fell there. But he had another horse, called 'Satan.' He need not have put such an apt title so far from him!

A few weeks after Drumclog, took place the Flodden of the Covenant, Bothwell Brig. What a sorrowful field it was! A field of deep anguish, wounds and death! Had it all been for the things of time and sense then certainly it was a field of woe and loss; but it was not that. Calvary is victory in every apparent Christian defeat. Amid the darkness, sweat, tears and blood, the sufferers there maybe could not see themselves as such, but they were more than conquerors through Him that loved them.

John Dick was in the struggle at Bothwell, but he escaped both wounding and the horrors exacted upon the Covenanters taken prisoner there. He was at liberty until the early autumn of 1683, when in his native city he was betrayed to the government by a poor woman. She was rewarded for this, but after his execution she was overcome with grief and lost her reason.

On 29 August 1683, he was brought before the Committee of Public Affairs. In his debate there with the bishop he had the better of him; but, being true to Jesus Christ, he was considered untrue to King Charles II. A fearful crime! Two days later, he stood in the Council and the substance of his examination was read to him. He made various comments upon it and gave his signature. On 4 September, with a miller from Linlithgow, George Lapsley, who was one of the wounded at Bothwell, and who had been in jail since 1681, he came before the Criminal Court, and was indicted for high treason. His own signed confession was read to him. Clear and plain his brave declaration meant his death sentence, but earnestly he urged that it might be added to in the confession, that it was

John Dick

his opinion that the blood of Presbyterians shed during the persecuting years, solely for their principles, was murder: and he asked that he might be allowed to conduct his own defence. His judges adamantly refused to accede to this and pronounced him guilty of high treason. The trial was completely closed, and he was sentenced to die by hanging in the Grassmarket on 28 September. He said to them, 'For you to pass such a sentence upon me without hearing me in my own defence is a practice never before paralleled even among heathen.' He would have gone on, but they were as whited walls to him. Ordered to stop, he was roughly taken from the court room with George Lapsley, also sentenced to death for high treason. They were then drawn away down the Canongate to the Tolbooth.

There were twenty-five prisoners in two big upper cells of the Canongate Tolbooth that September of 1683. Hardly anyone of these ever expected to be out in the open air again until he was taken out on his last journey up the hill of the High Street and down the 'Sanctified bends of the Bow' to the scaffold in the Grassmarket. But they were men of God, and they prayed for help planned well in the guidance given to make a mass escape. Even friends in the city and as far away as Glasgow knew the time and manner of it and prayed for good success.

One of the cells was above the other. Those in the lower one, on a certain night, were to begin to saw through the iron bars of their glassless window, while those in the room above were to get part of their flooring ready to take up easily when all the crossed irons were cut. Dropping down into the lower room, they could then all escape together.

At about nine o'clock one night the first bar was sawn through. To the horror of all concerned, before any of those at the window could catch it, down it fell into the narrow street below where a sentry was posted! They waited anxiously, watched and prayed. The continued silence gave them their greatly desired Amen; and they proved God, for, although their window was almost parallel with that of the garrison commander, Lord Linlithgow, who lived on the other side of the street, they had neither been heard nor seen; and the sentry on his beat had never seen the iron staunchion nor heard it fall. Next morning at about nine o'clock a friend was allowed in to visit them. They requested him, when he went out into the street again, to see if the window with its missing iron was noticeable to passers by. On going down, he found the bar and actually managed to get it sent in to them. They put it up to all intents and purposes firm in its place, and their deft eager hands, when opportunities were given, plied the saw through the remaining irons. When all was ready the signal was given to those above. Lifting up the loose part of their floor, one by one they dropped into the lower room. Through the barless window all the twenty-five of them got down into the street and disappeared into the night. Many of them were country-men who did not know their ways about the city, but all found safe haven. One of them, an Englishman, had the faith, or guided simplicity, to go forward and knock at the door of a house where he had seen a light in a window. It happened to be the home of the bishop! To the serving maid who came to the door he frankly told who he was. She took him in and hid him until she got him safely away to some Covenanter friends. Only one of the twenty-five was ever recaptured – John Dick, student of theology.

What a row broke out in the Edinburgh circles of official-dom! The magistrates of the city were called together and roundly and soundly blamed! They were warned that in the

John Dick

future they must see to the security of all prisoners in the Canongate Tolbooth or they themselves would be severely punished. Fierce General Dalziel, in a Council of War, examined the captain, lieutenants, sergeants, corporals and sentries of that eventful night. Warders, too, were closely questioned; but no one knew anything at all about the escape. All that could be done was to begin again to fill the empty cells with other captives. It was all very reminiscent of Herod's insane fury at the escape of Peter.

Soon after regaining his liberty, John Dick wrote his 'Testimony to the Doctrine, Worship, Discipline, and Government of the Church of Scotland and the Covenanted Work of Reformation in the Three Kingdoms.' According to Wodrow, it was, in his day, in everybody's hands; for, although John Dick had apparently meant it for his own private use, it was published by friends after his death, as a book of fifty-eight pages, and greatly valued.

Dr Robert Burns, editor of Wodrow's *History of the Sufferings*, refers particularly to those points in Dick's Paper directed towards a sense of sin and practical personal holiness: '1. Let there be a cordial endeavour in the strength of our blessed Master, as to strive against every sin without exception, so as to close with every commanded duty with delight. 2. I would offer for your exercise that indispensable duty of repentance, in exercising which I shall offer these few Christian advices: First, let us dig deep in this matter. Secondly: let us take a view of all our actual transgressions. Thirdly: let there be much singleness of heart in this matter. Fourthly: let there be much dependence on the Lord for grace. 3. Let there be the actual exercise of the grace, the noble and fountain grace of faith, as also of patience. 4. Let us fall effectually about preparing of ourselves to meet our blessed Lord and Master, whether as to His Coming for our delivery in time, or to judgment at that great day.' In John Dick personal piety and devoted service kept step together.

Free for about six months, he was taken again in the first days of March 1684. Quickly brought to trial, he declined to say anything about the grand escape, stood fast to his former declarations, was brought before the Justiciary on 4 March, and ordered to be hanged next day.

The young heart was strong and full, the mind clear and eager, the desire to live and minister so naturally hopeful; but his hours were now so few, the splendid task so nearly done though seemingly barely started, and God in His own peculiar way was setting apart him that was godly for Himself.

Graciously proved had been the saving power of Christ and Him crucified in John Dick's heart and life; and short enough and harassed had been the time of his proved preaching of the blood of the Lamb to others. Now, while the last grains of the sands of time continued to run through his hour-glass, he wrote letters tender, fervent and Christ-fragrant, to a few friends. That he was 'holy and blameless before Him in love' is their testimony. His last night in the world was wondrously like the one in which he yielded his all to the Lord. Now Redemption would soon be gloriously complete, and through eternity he would serve his Master and see His face. Intensely moving is the letter written by him to his father during his last hours:

Dear Sir,

This hath been one of the pleasantest nights I have had in my lifetime; the competition is only betwixt it and that I got eleven years ago, at Nesbit in Northumberland, where and when in a barley ridge upon the Saturday's night and Sabbath morning, before the last communion I did partake of in Ford church, the

John Dick

Lord firmly laid the foundation stone of grace in my heart, by making me with my whole soul close with Him upon His own terms, that is, to take Him to be my King, Priest, and Prophet, yea, to be my all in all, to renounce my own righteousness, which at the best is but as rotten rags, and to rest upon His righteousness alone for salvation; as also to give myself entirely without reserve, in soul, body, heart, affections, and the whole faculties of my soul, and powers of my body, to be by Him disposed at His pleasure, for the advancement of His glory, and the upbuilding of my own soul, and the souls of others; inserting this clause (being conscious to myself of great infirmity) that the fountain of free grace and love should stand open for me so long, and so oft as my case should call for it. This my transaction with my whole soul, without the least ground of suspicion of the want of sincerity, which I found had been amissing in endeavours of that nature formerly, now my blessed Lord helped me to, or rather made in me, and solemnised that night and morning ere I came off that ridge. I confirmed it no less than ten or twelve times, and the oftener I reiterated, the gale continued so fresh and vigorous, that I was forced to cry, 'Hold, Lord, for the sherd is like to burst': so that I hope my dearest Lord is now a-coming, and that the hands of Zerubbabel, who hath laid this foundation, is now about to finish it; and indeed He is now building very fast, for which my soul blesseth Him, desiring you may join with me in so necessary a work. I hope ere long the cope-stone shall be put on, the result of all which shall be praises and shouting to Him that sits upon the Throne, and to the Lamb throughout all the ages of eternity, of long-lasting eternity. This, with my earnest prayers while in the body, that the Lord would help you to mind His glory, and your own soul's eternal welfare, is all the legacy you can expect from him, who is both

Your Affectionate son, and Christ's prisoner,

JOHN DICK

PS: *I hope, ere I go Home, to get another sight of you. Let none see this till I be in my grave. The Lord gave me to you freely, so*

I entreat you, be frank in giving me to Him again, and the more free this be, the less cause you shall have to repent.

Young Erskine of Carnock, in his Journal, tells of how he accompanied his dear friend, John Dick, from the prison to the Grassmarket on 5 March 1684; and of how, as the crowds surged around the scaffold and the drums were deafening to hear, he looked down, and, says Erskine, 'I got a smile from him.' Brave, composed, ecstatic, full of faith and of the Holy Ghost, John Dick was going Home with joy. Amid the shameful drumming din he sang the 2nd Psalm,

> *Why rage the heathen? and vain things*
> *Why do the people mind?*

Ezekiel, chapter nine, was his reading, and among his last words were these, 'I am come here this day, and would not change my lot with the greatest in the world. I lay down my life willingly and cheerfully for Christ and His cause, and I heartily forgive all mine enemies. I forgive all them who gave me my sentence, and them who were the chief cause of my taking; and I forgive him who is behind me [the executioner]. I advise you who are the Lord's people, to be sincere in the way of godliness, and you who know little or nothing of the power thereof, to come to Him, and trust God, He will not disappoint you. I say trust in the Lord, and He will support or strengthen you in whatever trouble or affliction you may meet with. I remember, when Abraham was about to sacrifice his son, Isaac said, "Here is the wood, and the fire, but where is the sacrifice?"' The strong, young eyes gazed up intently at the gallows, then out across the crowds, and a light of adoration came upon his face. 'Now blessed be the Lord,' he said, 'here is the sacrifice and free-will offering. Adieu, farewell all friends.'

So went Home to His Father's House, John Dick, student

of theology, with an eager and glowing anticipation of the crown of righteousness bright upon him. What to him was absence from the body compared with the full presence of the Lord? Faithful keeper of the faith, sure runner in the race, and good soldier in the fight, he was a 'beloved of the Lord' cheerful giver who died that early Spring day in the Edinburgh Grassmarket.

Sang Henry Vaughan, the Welsh poet, both for himself and John Dick:

> *Lord, with what courage and delight*
> *I do each thing,*
> *When Thy least breath sustains my wing!*
> *I shine and move*
> *Like those above,*
> *And, with much gladness*
> *Quitting sadness,*
> *Make me fair days of every night.*

Donald Cargill

Donald Cargill

IN far-away Trans Himalaya there is an interesting little town
called Kargil. Its flat-roofed, mud-walled and stone-founded
houses are terraced high on the steep, rocky sides of the swift
and cold Suru River. It is on an important-enough trade route
between Kashmir, Tibet and Chinese Turkestan. Along its
thin straggling market-street pass Tibetans, Turkis, Chinese,
Ladakhis, Baltis, Kashmiris and Indians. It is certainly a strate-
gic centre for the spread of the Gospel with so many Budd-
hists, Moslems, Hindus and Sikhs passing to and fro, and some
of them travelling far. A word retained in a heart, or a Scripture portion in a wallet might be the beginning of saving
wonders in an otherwise unreachable place.

A few days' marches beyond Kargil lived and died that fine
Tibetan Christian, Yoseb Gergan, whose splendid feat in the

Donald Cargill

complete translation of the Old Testament, and the revision of the New Testament, into Tibetan is an outstanding Christian work of the twentieth-century. Through that meagre bazaar of Kargil were carried between Western Tibet and India, on their hazardous and long journeys across the bone-strewn snowy trails, the precious manuscripts, and eventually the proofs of the Book of God in the Tibetan tongue, 'A Holy Spirit translation.' Now copies of it are carried into Lhasa itself. Wycliffe and Tyndale are honoured names; and so is that of Gergan.

Sometimes while there in Kargil I thought of the similarity in sound of the name of the Central Asian town and that of Cargill – Donald Cargill, one of the mighty men of the Covenanters, 'a chief among the captains.'

It is one of Patrick Walker's classics, 'Some Remarkable Passages in the Life and Death of that Singular, Exemplary, Holy in Life, Zealous, and Faithful unto the Death, Mr Daniel Cargill . . . commonly called Donald Cargill.' Unique Patrick Walker! Covenanter indeed! Thumbscrew and Boot sufferer, Tolbooth prisoner and escapee, banished man, author, biographer and printer! Patrick the Pedlar! Said R.L.S. in one of his letters from Samoa, 'When I was a child, and indeed until I was nearly a man, I consistently read Covenanting books. Now that I am a grey beard – or would be if I could raise the beard – I have returned, and for weeks have read little else but Wodrow, Walker and Shields, etc. . . . My style is from the Covenanting writers.' The trio mentioned by that doyen of literature would hardly have considered this a compliment! It does praise their virile living writing, all the same.

Patrick Walker was just the very keenest assessor of spiritual values, and a man had to be truly spiritual for Patrick to call him so. Cargill satisfied his every deep and close examination, and every dear demand, and was to him first, last and always, and so now for us all, 'Blest Cargill.'

As Walker thought of Cargill and others like him, he wrote in exultant faith, 'And it hath been, is, and maybe comforting to all the Lord's people, that our Reformation in all the steps thereof, hath been of and for the Lord, in that He raised up, and continued such a succession of earnest contenders and faithful witnesses, through so many ages, that none have exceeded them since the apostles went off the stage.'

What a dividing-of-soul-and-spirit, convincing-of-sin, and converting-to-Christ preacher Cargill must have been! Patrick Walker says, for he was his glad hearer, and knew him intimately, 'He preached from experience and went to the experience of all that had any of the Lord's gracious dealings with their souls. It came from his heart and went to the heart; as I have heard some of our common hearers say, that he spake as never man spake, for his words went through them.'

One day some complained to Donald Cargill that his sermons were too short, and so also were his prayers. They said, 'It is long between meals, and we are in a starving condition. All is good, sweet and wholesome that you deliver; but why do you straiten us so much for shortness?' His reply was, 'Ever since I bowed a knee in good earnest to pray, I never durst pray and preach with my gifts; and where my heart is not affected, and comes not up with my mouth, I always thought it time for me to quit. What comes not from the heart, I have little hope that it will go to the heart of others . . . "Create in me a clean heart, O God; and renew a right spirit within me . . . Then will I teach transgressors thy ways, and sinners shall be converted unto thee." '

There was a disciplined life behind the gracious power of Cargill, and a close walk with God. He was a man who took

Donald Cargill

heed to himself and his ways. Buffeted by the devil, men, and circumstances, he hit straight and hard at his own body, making it his servant to do the will of God. Knowing whom he had believed, and the saving power of His precious blood, nevertheless, he also knew that there was a prize and a crown to be given by the Man of Calvary; and such were not to be received from His pierced hands by any except those who had His mind, and whose lives were akin to His. A castaway he would not be! The gleam of the incorruptible crown was ever around him.

One day, in a wood where he was hiding, Marion Weir brought him some food, and urged him to eat heartily. 'Let me alone,' he said to her. 'I cannot be pressed. I have not taken a meal these thirty years but what I could have taken as much when I arose as when I sat down.' Temperate in eating, we judge that he was temperate in all things. Patrick Walker says that one exhausting day he saw a man give him a drink of water out of his bonnet, and another drink out of the same dish between sermons; and, 'That was the best he got that day; and he had tasted nothing since morning.'

The godly pedlar liked to tell what Cargill's 'first note' was, what his texts were, and 'sententious sayings.' They were of one heart; and Patrick was a faithful reporter taking delight in the words of a master, setting down with joy such gems as, 'Those who know themselves best will fear themselves most'; and, 'No sooner has Christ become all in all to a soul, but the next wish of that soul is, "O that He were so to all the world!" '

Lovingly fresh and green the living colours remained, in the chastened mind of Patrick Walker, of the memorable Sabbath when Cargill ministered for the last time. He says, 'I had the happiness to hear blest Cargill preach his last public sermons [as I had several times before, for which, while I live, I desire to bless the Lord] in Dunsyre Common, between Clydesdale and Lothian, where he lectured upon the 1st Chapter of *Jeremiah* and preached upon that soul-refreshing text, *Isaiah* 26, the last two verses, "Come, my people, enter into your chambers," wherein he was short, marrowy and sententious, as his ordinary was in all his public sermons and prayers, with the greatest evidences of concernedness, exceeding all that ever I heard open a mouth, or saw open a Bible to preach the Gospel, with the greatest indignation at the unconcernedness of hearers.' Cargill spoke that day apparently knowing that his work was nearly done, and, continues his reverent listener, 'He insisted what kind of chambers these were of protection and safety, and exhorted us all earnestly to dwell in the clefts of the rock, to hide ourselves in the wounds of Christ, and to wrap ourselves in the believing application of the promises flowing therefrom, and to make our refuge under the shadow of His wings, until these sad calamities pass over, and the dove come back with the olive leaf in her mouth. These were the last words of his last sermon.' Blest Cargill, indeed!

Sir Robert Hamilton, the friend of James Renwick, says of Cargill, 'First, as he was of a most holy, strict, tender and compassionate practice and conversation, so he was affectionate, affable, and tenderhearted to all he judged had anything of the image of God in them; sober and temperate in his diet, saying commonly, "It was well won that was won of the flesh"; generous, liberal and most charitable to the poor, a great hater of covetousness, a frequent visitor of the sick, much alone, loving to be retired; but when about his Master's public work laying hold of every opportunity to edify; in converse still dropping what might minister grace to the hearers; his very countenance was edifying to beholders often sighing with deep groans;

Donald Cargill

preaching in season and out of season, upon all hazards, ever the same in judgment and practice.' Blest Cargill!

About the time that the Pilgrim Fathers were setting forth on their all-important journeys, in 1620, Donald Cargill was born in the Rattray and Cargill district of Perthshire beyond the source of the Tay. He spent most of his boyhood there, with some schooling in Aberdeen. Familiar with the hills and hollows of his childhood, he had to run very fast up and down them one day, years later, when chased by swift and armed pursuers who came to take him in his preaching. Cargill was always preaching. He ran for a known rocky chasm where the River Keith narrows. Mounting a huge rock he took a flying leap across the river. None of his hunters dared follow. They gave up the chase. It is called 'Cargill's Loup' to this day. Sometime later, a friend spoke to him about his great jump. He laughed and said that he had had to take a fifteen miles run before he could do it! All the way from Perth!

He studied philosophy at the University of St Andrews, town of legend and of truth. Andrew Lang pictures it for us.

> *St Andrews, by the Northern Sea,*
> *A haunted town it is to me!*
> *A little city, worn and grey,*
> *The grey North Ocean girds it round,*
> *And o'er the rocks, and up the bay,*
> *The long sea-rollers surge and sound.*
> *And still the thin and biting spray*
> *Drives down the melancholy street,*
> *And still endure and still decay,*
> *Towers that the salt winds vainly beat.*
> *Ghostlike and shadowy they stand,*
> *Dim mirrored in the wet sea-sand.*

It is the old grey town of Wishart and Knox; and of Ruther-ford and Halyburton who lie side-by-side within its walls.

While a student, Cargill, under conviction of sin, had some very distressing temptations. He got so low in them that more than once he went out with the object of taking away his own life ; but always some Providential circumstances prevented his doing so. One day, when intending to throw himself into an old disused coal pit, the words of the Saviour, 'Son, thy sins are forgiven thee,' powerfully spoke peace to his soul. He lived lifelong in their assuring grace.

His godly father was very eager that he should study divin-ity and become a minister of the Gospel; but Donald Cargill shrank from that, feeling that he had as yet no call to the ministry. The Holy Spirit dealt with him and put him into such an exercise that he decided to set time apart and wait upon the Lord in fasting and prayer, seeking guidance. With strong assurance to him was given the Scripture, *Ezekiel* 3.1: 'Son of man, eat that thou findest; eat this roll and go speak unto the house of Israel.' It was his call; and if ever one made full proof of it, he did. He ever made full proof of his ministry. When his studies were finished, the congregation of the Barony Kirk of Glasgow invited him there, and the first text that the Presby-tery asked him to preach on was his 'speaking word', *Ezekiel* 3.1!

On coming to the Barony Kirk, Cargill felt that the people were light and had little concern for the Word. He was dis-couraged at this and decided to return home. Godly ministers of the city asked him why he was going. He said, 'They are a rebellious people.' They tried to get him to change his mind but he was determined to go. Getting his horse, he went to the home of his friend, James Durham, the famous Covenanter minister and writer, of whom Spurgeon said, 'Whatever Dur-

Donald Cargill

ham has written is very precious ... Durham is a prince among spiritual expositors.' James Durham died at the early age of thirty-six, venturing his soul, as he said, upon *Matthew* 11.28. While he was saying farewell to friends in Durham's home, a prayerful woman said to Cargill, 'Sir, you have promised to preach on Thursday, and have you appointed a meal to a poor starving people, and will ye go away and not give it? If ye do the curse of God will go with ye.' Cargill sat down and asked her and the others to pray for him. He stayed. His ministry was a spiritual success, and he a blessing to all who knew him till King Charles II came home again, and the unhappy Restoration took place.

In 1660, 29, May was set apart to commemorate the return to the throne of Charles II. It was also the date of his birthday. It happened to be one of Cargill's usual preaching days. A thronging crowd filled the Barony Kirk. Coming into the pulpit, he looked across the great congregation, and said to them, 'We are not come here to keep this day upon the account for which others keep it. We thought once to have blessed the day wherein the king came home again; but now we think we should have reason to curse it. And if any of you be come here in order to the solemnising of this day we desire you to remove.' Patrick Walker tells that he spoke with tears. 'The unhappy Restoration,' he writes, 'when hell, Rome, and all their proselytes and favourites had their invention upon the rack, in their wicked crafty counsels, how to stop and overturn our great covenanted work of Reformation!'

Vigilant saints of the Most High, Cargill, McWard and some others met to pray before the Restoration. Patrick Walker says, 'Mr McWard was the first that prayed with more than ordinary enlargement and gale upon his spirit, earnestly begging of the Lord that, in mercy, love and pity, He would seal,

spirit and fit a remnant to stand steadfast whatever and whatsoever direction the winds might blow; and that there might be a
succession of faithful witnesses raised up to follow the Lord
fully in life and death.' It was an abundantly-answered prayer
with Cargill part of the answer; Cargill of the fixed heart
whose over twenty years of trials began when he refused to
say welcome to an enemy of God – Charles II, when he came
home again. From then on his life is a record of unrelenting
searches for him, pitiless chases after him, incredible escapes,
exhausting wanderings, and he in utter holiness shining
through all as he prayed, preached and laboured, a saved sinner displaying the wondrous grace of God in Christ Jesus, 'a
man greatly beloved indeed.'

Cargill gave himself to prayer and to the ministry of the
Word. Says his faithful biographer, 'From his youth he was
much given to secret prayer, yea, whole nights, and it was
observed by some both in families and when in secret, he always sat straight upon his knees, without resting upon anything, with his hands lifted up and some took notice that he
died the same way with the bloody rope about his neck.' 'Mr
Cargill, the next Sabbath preached at Cairntable between
Loudon and Tweedale, in his wounds and blood: for no danger nor distress could stop him in going about doing good, and
distributing food to so many starving souls up and down the
land, his time being short, that so he might finish his course
with joy. He preached that day upon that text, "And what shall
I more say, for the time would fail me to speak of Gideon and
Jephthah." At night some said to him, "We think, Sir, praying
and preaching go best with you when danger and distress is
greatest." He said that it had been so, and he hoped that it
would be so.'

In prophetic vision, Walker places him with Alexander

Donald Cargill

Peden, saying 'By these foregoing relations all may see that these two servants of Christ, Mr Cargill and Mr Peden, were clear-sighted in what they did foresee and tell.'

The evils and cruelties of these times broke the hearts of some and unsettled the minds of others so that amongst the Covenanters some ran into serious extremes. Bands of sad people called the Sweet Singers mournfully paced the streets plaintively singing Psalms 74, 79, 80, 83, and 137. These so described things as they were. Says Dr King Hewison, 'Grief was assuaged by cursings; joy was intensified by prayer; fasting increased both faith and sorrow'. The blood of the devout martyrs Potter and Stewart was flaunted on a handkerchief. Utter abject helplessness for some became utter despair.

Then arose 'muckle John Gibb', a giant of a man, a sailor. He would deliver the people of God and destroy all their enemies. How? Retire to the hills and fast, sing and pray, and wait to see God in His justice and holy wrath destroy by fire the wicked city of Edinburgh. And they themselves would help to bring it about by becoming as perfect as it was possible for Christians to be. They became 'ascetics, despisers of home comforts, destroyers of Bibles having human addenda, such as metrical psalms, chapters, verses, pictures, prefaces, printers' marks – burners of the Covenants and relative documents, repudiators of the king and his officials, of educated clergy, of the calendar and its terminology, and of every imaginable thing, even to the fashions of men.' They gave up all except life itself which was kept in them by bread and water only. They paid no attention to the word of any man, and would read nothing but the pure text of the Bible. The leading colleague of John Gibb was David Jamie whom Patrick Walker called 'a good scholar lost and a minister spoilt'.

Cargill had the Gibbites much on his heart and longed for their restoration. He felt, as did Patrick Walker, that they laid 'far more weight and stress upon the duties of prayer, fasting and mourning than upon Christ's satisfaction, obedience and intercession,' and actually besought them to let him speak to them from the 37th Psalm and from it interpreting for them what he felt was the will of the Holy Spirit for their most trying times. John Gibb would not allow this but agreed to Cargill coming to see them. Patrick Walker says, 'There was a bed made for him and John Gibb: he lay down a little but rose in haste, and went to the muir all night; I well remember it was a cold easterly wet fog. Many waiting on him to have his thoughts about them, he refused upon the Sabbath evening to give his thoughts about them. They found him in the muir in the morning wet and cold, and very melancholy, wanting rest all night and great grief upon his spirit.' Later the whole band of the Gibbites were taken by dragoons and put into prison where their behaviour shocked Covenanter fellow-prisoners, some of whom were under sentence of death. John Gibb, David Jamie, and two women, were banished to America where the one lived among the Red Indians and the other became a clerk in New York and quite a religious man.

In the last paragraph of The National Covenant are these words, 'We call the Living God, the searcher of our hearts, to witness, who knoweth this to be our sincere desire, and un-feigned resolution, as we shall answer to Jesus Christ at the great day, and, under the pains of God's everlasting wrath, and of infamy and loss of all honour and respect in the world.' They were vessels of fragile human clay who framed and read the solemnly binding words of that, one of the greatest docu-ments ever compiled among men, and penned their small names at the close of it; but in their hearts was the knowledge of God through Jesus Christ, and they triumphed in His power. Such was Donald Cargill.

Severely wounded at Bothwell, Cargill was taken prisoner; but his captors let him go again on seeing who he was. Such was the respect of some for him and the ministry. Recovering from his wounds, he went to Holland and returned in a few months. He resided in South Queensferry until early June 1680, when he and the valiant and good Henry Hall of Haughhead were surprised by the armed Governor of Blackness Castle and his party. There was a struggle, and Henry Hall gave his own life to let Cargill get away sorely hurt. He crawled into a dark corner and lay there until he was found, says Patrick Walker, by 'a very ordinary woman who cared for him,' and that 'afterwards there was a change in her for the better.'

In the leather bag left upon Cargill's horse, or in possession of Hall, was found what, ever afterwards, is known as 'The Queensferry Paper.' Hall and Cargill were formulating this paper, and it would soon have been made public. It was recognised by the Covenanters and was adhered to by martyrs and the banished as in all things agreeable to the Word of God.

The literature and letters of the banished Covenanters are a study in themselves. These men and women went forth very brave, but with heavy hearts for those they left behind; as some wrote, 'Now, Dear Friends, we shall shut up these few preceding lines, confused as they are, for we are confused, by reason of soldiers who are continually with us within the prison. And now we desire to be minded of you, and who intend through the strength of Him who only can enable us, to be mindful of you; yea, we shall say, if we forgot thee, O poor Zion, poor oppressed remnant of the Church of Scotland, then let our right hands forget their cunning and let our tongues cleave to the roof of our mouths. I say, if we forget you, O ye the poor persecuted remnant whom we are leaving behind, who are in the clefts of the rocks, and the secret places of the stairs. O remember Him who is calling to you that ye may let Him hear your voices and see your countenances ... Thus we leave you, dear friends, wives, children, and families, on the Hand of Him who is a Husband to the widow, a stay to the orphan, and a hiding place to His people, and the shadow of a great rock in a weary land; to whom be glory forever. Amen.' Twenty-three signatures were appended to that. Wodrow tells something of their severe trials on the voyage to be sold as slaves in Carolina.

> *Sing, then sing, ye solemn surges!*
> *Shout thy thunders, mighty main!*
> *Ours is but a light affliction,*
> *Fitting us for Glory's strain;*
> *When we meet our slaughtered kindred,*
> *With the Lamb who once was slain.*

*

In the last few weeks of the stirring life of Richard Cameron, Cargill was much with him, and supported him in his last Sabbath of preaching. Next Sabbath, unafraid, out in the open, wanderers who had so recently been urged by the Lion of the Covenant to be still and know that Jehovah was God, were now urged by Cargill to know that one of His princes and leaders had fallen among them. Cargill was very moved as he spoke of his friend. The young man, valorous beyond the telling, was dear to the veterans Cargill and Peden. They both in his death wore 'garments of praise for the spirit of heaviness'; but 'Puir Auld Sandie' could not refrain from leaving

Donald Cargill

his lair, and finding his way across the moors to lonely Ayrs-moss, he cast himself down upon the grave of the beloved slain, crying lovingly and longingly, 'O tae be wi' ye, Richie! O tae be wi' ye, Richie!'

His time and that of Cargill had not yet come. It was hastening on. One day Peden kindly put his hand on the shoulder of John Wilson, who, a very few years later, was hanged in the Edinburgh Grassmarket, and said to him, 'Encourage yourself in the Lord, and follow fast, John; for ye will win up yonder shortly, and get on a' yir braws' [all your best and most beautiful clothes]. How often the Master must have said that to Peden and Cargill in their last few years [*Revelation* 7. 13–17].

The fires of persecution continued to be heated seven-fold; and the testimony of the sufferers was that of old, one of the highest of all testimonies, 'He will deliver us out of thine hand, O king. But if not, be it known unto thee, O king, we will not serve thy gods.' As their ranks thinned, they formed in more closely round the Cross. Their use of carnal weapons availed them very little; but their use of spiritual ones was mighty through God to the pulling down of strongholds. And Cargill was leader among them.

In his great book, *A Hind Let Loose*, Alexander Shields says, 'Now remained Mr Donald Cargill, deprived of his faithful colleague, destitute of his brethren's concurrence, but not of the Lord's counsel and conduct; by which he was prompted and helped to prosecute the testimony against the universal apostasy of the church and nation . . . for the sins especially of rulers who had arrived to the height of heaven-daring insolence in all wickedness . . . owned also by pro-fessors, not only as magistrates, but as members of the Christ-ian and Protestant Church; and that, however both the defensive arms of men had been used against them, and the Christian arms of prayer, and the ministerial weapon of preaching, yet that of ecclesiastical censure had not been authoritatively exerted against them. Therefore, that no weapon which Christ allows His servants under His standard to manage against His enemies might be wanting, though he could not obtain the concurrence of his brethren to strengthen the solemnity and formality of the action, yet he did not judge that defect, in this broken case of the church, could disable his authority, nor demur the duty, but that he might and ought to proceed to excommunication.'

Excommunication as practised through the centuries by the corrupt, unscriptural Church of Rome has no spiritual significance at all. It means nothing. It is in word only and not in power. By true men it is laughed at. 'That which is of the flesh is flesh,' and can never be anything else. Excommunication spiritual is something very different. The Torwood Excommunication had many evidences of being that.

In September, 1680, at Torwood, near Falkirk, before a great concourse of people, Cargill preached on *Ezekiel* 21. 25–27. He gave a short discourse 'On the nature, the subject, the causes, and the ends of excommunication in general; and then declared,' says Shields, 'that he was not led out of any private spirit or passion to this action, but constrained by conscience of duty, and zeal to God to stigmatize with this brand and wound with the sword of the Lord, these enemies of God that had so apostatised, rebelled against, mocked, despised, and defied our Lord, and to declare them, as they are none of His, to be none of ours . . . I being a minister of Jesus Christ, and having authority and power from Him, do in His Name, and by His Spirit, excommunicate, cast out of the true church, and deliver up to Satan, King Charles II . . .

Donald Cargill

James, Duke of York . . . James, Duke of Monmouth . . .
John, Duke of Rothes . . . Sir George Mackenzie . . . and
Thomas Dalziel of Binns.' The piled-up lawful reasons for
this tremendous act were given in every case with Cargill
believing that what he had bound on earth would be bound
in heaven.

A large reward was offered by King and Government for
this man – 'One of the most seditious preachers, a villainous
and fanatical conspirator.' He continued to preach, ever
redeeming his time. The wanderers' martyr-lists lengthened.
Cargill corresponded with prisoners under sentence of death,
such as James Skene, aristocrat in the flesh and in the spirit,
who wrote from 'My delectable prison; in which my Lord
has allowed me His peace and presence, and comforted me
with that I shall reign with Him eternally; for I am His, and
bought with His precious blood.' And 'From my Lord Jesus,
His house, which He has made a sweet palace, wherein He
shows me His wonderful free love; the close prison above the
Iron House, in the High Tolbooth of Edinburgh, 1680. PS I
told the Chancellor the cause was just, whereby the king and
others were excommunicated at the Torwood; though I was
not there, yet I adhered to it.' And again 'PS I got my sum-
mons for eternity with sound of trumpet yesternight; and my
indictment with five shouts of the trumpet, and pursuivants
in their coats, at seven of the clock, was a grave sight, but my
Lord helped me not to be afraid at it, since all was from Him.'
He was a choice soul, James Skene. The day before he died,
he wrote, 'I am going to a mansion of glory that my Lord
has prepared for me. I shall have a crown of life; because I
have been, by my blessed Lord's assistance – though I slipped
aside – made faithful to the death.' He came from Aberdeen
where Rutherford penned most of his seraphic lines. It almost

seems as if he had been looking on over Samuel Rutherford's shoulder.

> *We shall rise above Dunnottar,*
> *Rise above the sounding sea;*
> *Rise above the western moorlands,*
> *Glorious, beautiful and free;*
> *Meet in cloud of light the Bridegroom*
> *None so beautiful as He!*
> *He shall say, "Arise, my fair one!"*
> *And the shades shall flee away,*
> *And the sleep of death be broken,*
> *And the grave be light as day.*
> *And the Sunshine of the 'ages*
> *Never ending' round us play.*

So runs to its close, *The Song of the Prisoners*, by George Paulin.

*

Cargill went to England for three months, when, says Patrick Walker, 'The Lord blessed his labours in the ministry to the conviction and edification of many souls.' There were brave English hearts among those who took the Covenant, and in the grey northern land far from their homes some gave their all for Christ, such as Colonel Rumbold, ex-Cromwellian soldier, who contended that no man was born into the world with a saddle on his back, neither was there born another with spurs on his feet to ride him! His death was a cruel one; but he died saying that if every one of his grey hairs was a life, he would give them all for the Lord Jesus Christ.

Cargill returned to Scotland in April 1681, and gave himself to constant preaching. He gave his last message at Dunsyre, near Lanark, on 10 July. That night, asleep in bed at Covington Mill, he was taken prisoner with the young men,

Donald Cargill

Walter Smith and James Boig. The rude accounts of their capture given by the authorities accord but ill with that given by young, soon-to-die, Walter Smith, who wrote, 'We were singularly delivered by Providence into the adversaries' hand, and, from what I could learn, were betrayed by none, nor were any accessory to our taking more than we ourselves, and particularly let none blame the Lady of St John's Kirk in this.' She attended Covenanter meetings. Patrick Walker did blame her. He felt that she had plenty of time to send word to Covington Mill while her own house was being searched.

For fear of rescue, their captors, Irvine of Bonshaw and his troop, hurried them away through Lanark, Glasgow and on to Edinburgh. In Lanark, the three were tied fast on bareback horses. Bonshaw himself tied Cargill's feet very hard below the horse's belly. The Covenanter looked down at him and asked, 'Why do you tie me so hard?' Then he sadly added, 'Your wickedness is great. You will not long escape the just judgment of God; and if I am not mistaken, it will seize upon you in this place.' It did! Next year he got his reward. 'The price,' says Patrick Walker, 'of innocent blood, precious blood, dear blood, blood that cries both loud and long!' Coming to Lanark, 'he and one of his cursed comrades fell afighting,' and in the fight Bonshaw was thrust through and died of his wounds.

Cargill appeared before several courts, and on 26 July was sentenced to die next day with Walter Smith and James Boig, students of theology, William Thomson, servant, and William Cuthill, seaman. The members of 'the Council were very fierce and furious against Cargill,' says Patrick Walker, 'especially Chancellor Rothes,' and he records, 'Rothes raged against him ... Rothes threatened him with extraordinary torture and violent death.' Donald Cargill, looking at Rothes, said, 'My Lord Rothes, forbear to threaten me; for die what death I will, your eyes shall not see it; and 'tis well known to some yet alive that he died that morning that Mr Cargill, and those worthies with him, suffered in the afternoon.'

After the Council meeting, Rothes took very ill. He sent his wife, Countess Rothes who favoured the Good Old Cause, for one of her Covenanter ministers, saying that his own were good to live with but not to die with. Two Covenanters, John Carstairs and George Johnston, came to him. 'Carstairs,' says Patrick Walker, 'dealt very faithfully and freely with him, rehearsing many wicked acts of his life; to whom he said, "We all thought little of what that man did in excommunicating us, but I find that sentence binding upon me now, and will bind to all eternity." ' There were noblemen there. Continues Patrick Walker, 'Rothes roaring so loud under the horror of conscience for his active wicked life in persecuting, made these noblemen leave him, weeping. William Duke of Hamilton said, "We banish these men from us, and yet when dying we call for them. This is melancholy work." '

The five condemned received their sentence with trumpet blast. Said Cargill, 'That's a weary sound, but the sound of the last trumpet will be a joyful sound to me, and all that will be found having on Christ's righteousness.'

The Cloud of Witnesses for the Royal Prerogatives of Jesus Christ, comparable with *The Scots Worthies*, must be one of the greatest books of martyrology ever published. Surely it is right that it should open with 'Donald Cargill,' chronologically taken out of position though the account be, to lead the life-stories of witnesses – ministers, weavers, tailors, labourers, serving-men, serving-maids, noblemen and noble-women, farmers and others from all walks of life, through its more than six hundred pages. Smith and Boig follow Cargill in honoured place.

William Cuthill from the Forth seaport, Borrowstouness, familiarly known as Bo'ness, wrote a long preamble about things relative to his times, followed by pages of his own personal testimony, as from 'One ready to step into Eternity . . . One of Christ's sufferers.' He closes requesting 'All to bear with faults of weakness, especially when the sword of the adversary is above a man's head'; and he takes farewell of the world and all things in it saying, 'Welcome, Lord Jesus Christ; into Thy hands I commend my spirit.'

The serving man from Fife, William Thomson, was asked during his trial if to save his life he would say 'God save the king.' His answer to that was, 'I shall not beg my life at so dear a rate as to commit sin.' In his testimony he made very clear, what every other Covenanter did, too, that is, plainly show that he was ready to die for what he had been condemned, and that he was more a Covenanter than his judges had ever thought him to be. Following his pages of witness against evil man and devil, he closes by recommending the Cross of Christ, saying, 'I think they want a good bargain of it that want it, and I think they want nothing that have it, and get leave to carry it heartsomely and His Presence under it; I would advise you all to take it on. I dare say this much for your encouragement, that it is easy and sweet.'

The students of theology, Walter Smith and James Boig, made out short beautifully-written testimonies. Of Walter Smith, his old Dutch professor said that he exceeded all that he ever taught, and 'He was capable to teach many, but few to instruct him.' In Patrick Walker's *Six Saints of the Covenant*, there is a letter from Walter Smith to Janet Fimerton, 'Who feared lest she had not fled out of herself to Christ for righteousness.' Walker says, 'She was esteemed a singular Christian, of deep exercises, high attainments, and great experience in the serious and solid practice of godliness.' She later was a prisoner in Dunnottar Castle, and died at sea, one of a hundred, of whom twenty-four were women, going to New Jersey as slaves. She was taken prisoner the night that she and other friends tried to bury the bodies of John Watt, Robert Semple, and young Gabriel Semple, aged eighteen years.

In his testimony, Walter Smith said, 'I have no bitterness or malice at any living, so that what I am dying for, I am solidly and firmly persuaded to be truth and duty, according to my mean capacity . . . Beware of going back. Wait for Him. Be not anxious about what shall become to you, or the remnant; He is concerned; His intercession is sufficient.' He must have loved books greatly. Even in his last lines he persists in telling what books are good for anxious souls. He closes, 'I can get no more written, nor see I great need for it; for the testimonies of martyrs are not your rule. Farewell.' The Scriptures were their rule, both theirs and his.

James Boig addressed his testimony to his brother. Glory to God,' he says, 'who hath not been wanting to me in giving assistance, yea, many times unsought; and He is yet continuing and I hope shall do so to the end, to carry me above the fear of death, so that I am in as sweet a calm, as if I were going to be married to one dearly beloved. Alas! my cold heart is not able to answer His burning love; but what is wanting in me is, and shall be, made up in a Saviour complete and well furnished in all things, appointed of the Father for this end, to bring His straying children to their own Home, whereof, I think I may venture to say it, I am one, though worthless.

'Now I have no time to enlarge, else I would give you a more particular account of God's goodness and dealing with

Donald Cargill

me; but let this suffice, that I am once fairly on the way, and within the view of Immanuel's Land, and in hopes to be received an inhabitant there within the space of twenty-six hours at most.' Time was as precious to him as to Walter Smith. 'I have no more spare time. Grace, mercy and peace be with you. Amen.' He sets out too the Divine order for himself, 'Welcome, cross; welcome, gallows; welcome, Christ; welcome, heaven, and everlasting happiness.'

Donald Cargill wrote a long testimony. It was taken from him the day before he suffered. A loyal brave heart got pen, ink and paper into his cell during the last night. He left a further short testimony of a few paragraphs, the smallest of the five, beginning, 'This is the most joyful day that ever I saw in my pilgrimage on earth. My joy is now begun which I see shall never be interrupted . . . It is nearly thirty years since He made it sure . . . I have followed holiness, I have taught truth, and I have been most in the main things . . . This day I am to seal with my blood all the truths that ever I preached . . . I had a great sweetness of spirit and great submission as to my taking, the Providence of God was so eminent in it; and I could not but think that God judged it necessary for His glory to bring me to such an end, seeing he loosed me from such a work . . .' That neither king nor pope is head of the Church but Christ and Christ alone, the Scriptures say. So also said Donald Cargill; and in the last few lines he ever wrote, graphically expressed his horror at its being made an essential of the crown. James Renwick, who saw Cargill die, called this—Christ's Headship of the Church— 'The Uncommunicable Prerogative of Jehovah,' and died for it too.

There is no record of any word that the faithful-unto-death Boig, Thomson, and Cuthill said upon the scaffold, 'except that when one of them was singing his last song to the Lord,' Cargill stood ready waiting, the first to die. He stood with his back to the gallows and asked the multitude for their attention. He sang the 118th Psalm, beginning at verse 16.

> *The right hand of the mighty Lord*
> *exalted is on high;*
> *The right hand of the mighty Lord*
> *doth ever valiantly.*

Smiling, he looked up to the many people watching from their windows and asked them to listen to him for a few minutes. He was much interrupted by the drums and at times had to stop. He said that he was sure of his 'interest in Christ and peace with God as all within this Bible and Spirit of God can make me; and I am no more terrified at death, nor afraid of hell, because of sin, than if I had never sinned; for all my sins are freely pardoned and washed thoroughly away, through the precious blood and intercession of Jesus Christ . . . Be not discouraged at the way of Christ and the cause for which I lay down my life, and step into eternity, where my soul shall be as full of Him as it can desire to be.'

His faithful chronicler, Patrick Walker, lovingly and proudly tells, 'When he came to the scaffold and foot of the ladder, he blessed the Lord with uplifted hands, that he was thus near the crown; and when setting his foot upon the ladder to go up to embrace the bloody rope, he said, "The Lord knows I go up this ladder with less fear, confusion or perturbation of mind, than ever I entered a pulpit to preach."'

Walter Smith said that he was praying that 'All who are in His way may be kept from sinning under suffering.' He stooped down and said his farewells to his relations and acquaintances and the Church of God, and beckoning to the vast crowds said, 'Farewell also.' Once up the ladder, he said,

Donald Cargill

'Farewell, all created enjoyments, pleasures and delights; farewell, sinning and suffering; farewell, praying and believing, and welcome, heaven and singing. Welcome, joy in the Holy Ghost; welcome, Father Son and Holy Ghost; into Thy hands I commend my spirit.'

The napkin was put upon his face. He lifted it again, saying, 'I have one word more to say, and that is, to all that have any love to God and His righteous cause, that they will set time apart, and sing a song of praise to the Lord, for what He has done to my soul, and my soul says, "To Him be the praise." '

The New Song, 'Worthy is the Lamb that was slain,' is new now, and forever will be new. Walter Smith was singing it on the scaffold. Continues Patrick Walker, 'Mr Smith, as he did cleave to him, Donald Cargill, in love and unity in life, so he died with his face upon his breast; next Mr Boig, then William Cuthill and William Thomson; these five worthies hung all on one gibbet at the Cross of Edinburgh, on that never-to-be-forgotten bloody day, 27 July 1681 . . . The hangman hashed and hagged off all their heads with an axe. Mr Cargill's, Mr Smith's, and Mr Boig's heads were fixed upon the Netherbow Port; William Cuthill's and William Thomson's upon the West Port.'

> *Give me, my God! a heart as mild*
> *And plain, as when I was a child.*
> *That when Thy Throne is set, and all*
> *These conquerors before it fall,*
> *I may be found preserved by Thee,*
> *Amongst that chosen company,*
> *Who by no blood here overcame*
> *But the Blood of the Blessed Lamb.*

Epilogue

What were their losses, and what their gains? Their losses were themselves and all that they had. Their gains were great, not for themselves but for posterity. They, with their fellows, the Puritans, gained freedom in every realm of human living, thus winning and preserving democracy, and the right spiritually and morally to worship God with an open Bible interpreted by all. They were the pioneers of the Protestant intellectual renaissance, resulting in the discovery of so much for the good of man in his earth environment, accompanied by laws for the community in social ameliorations whose good can never be calculated. All by-products of the Gospel had to have a preserved Gospel. They were the preservers. They made possible the lawfulness of dissent in times of error, coldness and ecclesiastical death; cleared the way and dug the foundations of every religious revival we have since known, and were the first in the missionary enterprise. To them we owe our way of life, our constitution, our institutions, our commonwealth, and our honoured place among the nations of the world. But for them our place and that of the U.S.A., would have been low down among the Romanist nations with the grimly-attendant dire consequences of such a plight, the menace of atheistic Communism.

Their faith held no lifeless opinions. It was as spiritual and evangelical as they themselves were, alive unto God, taken up with the Person of the Lord Jesus Christ. So dear is their memory, so sure their testimony, that for us it must be: 'Whose faith follow, considering the end of their manner of life, Jesus Christ the same yesterday, and to-day, and forever.'

An outline of Scottish 'Covenant History' in the 17th century

THE story of religious covenanting in Scotland covers a long period, beginning in 1557 when certain men did 'band thame selfis' to maintain 'the trew preaching of the Evangell of Jesus Christ'. Two years later, after the return of John Knox from Geneva, the reforming party entered into three distinct covenants [at Perth, Edinburgh and Stirling respectively] for the purpose of promoting the work of the Reformation. Again, in 1560, a covenant of a more political nature contributed to the extirpation of French influence from Scottish affairs and issued within a few weeks in the Treaty of Edinburgh with Protestant England. Seven years later Mary of Scots was overthrown, and certain 'articles', to which the leaders of the people subscribed, virtually formed a still further 'band' to enable Protestantism to become 'rooted, grounded and settled' in the land.

These various covenants were eclipsed in interest and importance by another of 1581, sometimes called 'The King's Confession' and sometimes 'The Second Confession of Faith', which vigorously denounced Romish corruptions and clarified Protestant doctrine. The dread inspired by the approach of the Spanish Armada in 1588 moved King James VI and 'divers of his Estates' to enter into another covenant known as 'The General Band', and during the next four or five years, still further covenants concerning king, country and religion saw the light. More important, however, from the spiritual standpoint was a covenant promoted by the General

An outline of Scottish 'Covenant History'

Assembly of the Scottish Kirk in 1596, for this made the Little Kirk of Edinburgh a very Bochim, the like of which had not been seen in Scotland since the Reformation.

A new and ominous factor in political and religious life appeared in the early 17th Century. It had not been entirely absent during the late 16th Century, but after James VI's accession to the English throne in 1603 as James I, it increased in strength and importance, and ere long resulted in a long-drawn-out campaign between Episcopacy and Presbyterianism. The first two Stuart kings of England accepted wholeheartedly the pattern of episcopal church government as found in Scotland's southern neighbour, and Charles I in particular, urged on by Canterbury's infamous Archbishop William Laud, determined to make Scotland bow willy-nilly to the episcopal yoke. Came the tremendous storm of July, 1637, the ominous stool-throwing by Jenny Geddes, with the cry, 'Will ye read that book [the Prayer Book] in my lug?', the signing of the highly significant National Covenant in Greyfriars Church and Churchyard, the two Bishops' Wars extending to 1641, and, in general, the revolt of an entire nation against its rulers. The underlying cause was spiritual rather than political. A nation had queried the claim by a monarch to determine the form of government of a national church, and had fired a cannon whose sound reverberated to the farthest Hebrides.

The National Covenant of 1638, THE outstanding covenant of Scottish History, declared the firm determination of its Presbyterian authors and subscribers to resist to the death the claims of the King and his minions to override the Crown Rights of the Redeemer in His Kirk. It is a formidable document indeed, bristling with references to former Acts of Parliament in typical legal fashion. It gives high honour to the eternal God and His most holy Word; demands the faithful preaching of that Word, the due and right ministration of the sacraments, the abolishing of all false religion, and the rooting out of the king's empire of all heretics and enemies to the true worship of God, on conviction 'by the true Kirk of God'. The subscribers further say that they fear neither 'the foul aspersions of rebellion, combination, or what else our adversaries from their craft and malice would put upon us, seeing what we do is so well warranted, and ariseth from an unfeigned desire to maintain the true worship of God, the majesty of our King, and the peace of the kingdom, for the common happiness of ourselves and our posterity. They pledge themselves as in the sight of God to 'be good examples to others of all godliness, soberness, and righteousness, and of every duty we owe to God and man'.

The Covenant draws to a close with the following statement: 'That this our union and conjunction may be observed without violation, we call the LIVING GOD, THE SEARCHER OF OUR HEARTS, to witness, who knoweth this to be our sincere desire and unfeigned resolution, as we shall answer to Jesus Christ in the great day, and under the pain of God's everlasting wrath, and of infamy and loss of all honour and respect in this world: most humbly beseeching the LORD to strengthen us by His HOLY SPIRIT for this end, and to bless our desires and proceedings with a happy success; that religion and righteousness may flourish in the land, to the glory of GOD, the honour of our King, and peace and comfort of us all'.

The Kirk of Scotland had spoken; let the King and the Archbishop tremble. The King, however, chose to follow his own pre-determined policy and such devices as Laud could invent. Meanwhile his troubles in his realm of England reached their desperate climax. Civil War commenced in the summer of 1642 and Scotland and the English Long Parliament came into close co-operation. In the opinion of both alike, absolute monarchy was threatening the true interests of the children of God and the unique Lordship of the King of kings, and must be resisted at all costs. Within a year came the signing of The Solemn League and Covenant by the two peoples, in which the Convention of Scottish Estates, with the approval of the General Assembly of the Kirk, undertook to give the English Parliament military aid against the King, while the English Parliament on its part undertook to establish and enforce Presbyterianism in England and to meet the expenses of a Scottish army operating in England.

The events of the Civil War and Commonwealth periods we need not here discuss. Oliver Cromwell, 'the great Independent', emerged from the period of conflict as a semi-dictator; Scotland and England fell apart, not without war, only to be brought together again politically by the union of Parliaments which England enforced after its military triumph. But England as a nation soon tired of Puritan domination and in 1660 the son of Charles returned to rule England and Scotland as Charles II; he claimed to be in the eleventh year of his reign.

The new king's conscience was exceedingly pliable. In 1650, a year and a half after his father's execution, when he was using all endeavours to recover the two thrones, he had offered to subscribe and swear the National Covenant and the Solemn League and Covenant, and actually did so on the 23rd June. A month later he had accepted the Dunfermline Declaration, in which he deplored his father's opposition to the work of religious Reformation, confessed his mother's [Henrietta Maria's] Popish idolatry, professed his own sincerity and detestation of all 'Popery, superstition and idolatry, together with Prelacy' and all other errors and heresies, and announced his determination not to tolerate them in any part of his dominions. If royal promises are good, the outlook for Scotland, not to say England, was bright with hope. At a Coronation ceremony at Scone on New Year's Day, 1651, Charles renewed his oath and subscription to the 1638 and 1643 covenants. But the word of the son was no more reliable than that of the father, and when Charles found that he could not stand against the power of the English New Model army on the embattled field and that it was necessary for him to 'go on his travels again', he soon abandoned his solemn vows and drowned the voice of his conscience in the wine of forgetfulness.

The Restoration of Charles II in 1660 soon led to a full display of the King's perfidy and marked the commencement of the Covenanter Period proper. The fair promises contained in the Declaration of Breda in 1659 were virtually annulled by the astute Edward Hyde (Lord Clarendon), now acting as the lord chancellor of England, who contrived the inclusion of a qualification in each royal concession, to the effect that the king would agree to whatsoever Parliament proposed on each point of the Declaration. In this fashion Charles could make pretence of yielding to Parliament's desires while making sure, in the devious ways open to his ministers, that those desires were to all intents and purposes his own.

Acts of Parliament shortly restored the royal prerogative and supremacy in matters of religion. The National Covenant of 1638 and the Solemn League and Covenant of 1643 were condemned as high treason, and henceforward it became perilous to adhere to them or to speak with approval of them. Simultaneously came the news to Scotland that the king was set upon restoring prelacy in full strength and vigour. An obsequious Parliament at Edinburgh passed an Act to give effect to this resolve. In the Preamble of the Act is was asserted that the king possessed an 'inherent right', 'by virtue of his royal prerogative and supremacy in causes ecclesiastical', to legislate for the Kirk. The current oath of allegiance to the Crown tied all who took it to the same principle, namely, that whatever power the King claimed in Church and State was his of divine right.

Nor was this the limit of the matter. The evil system of patronage which had been abolished in 1649 was restored. This meant that patron and bishop, and no others, had authority in the presentation of ministers to livings. All ministers who had entered upon a living since 1649 but had not obtained such presentation were required to quit their parishes. Between three and four hundred men were thus sequestered.

In 1664, by Royal Prerogative, the Court of High Commission, which, together with the Star Chamber, had been Archbishop Laud's notorious instrument of repression, was again set up, with power to determine all aspects of Church policy. These measures gave the bishops legal authority to hunt down all who refused to conform to their demands. Non-conformists—and all true Covenanters were such—were savagely persecuted during the next twenty-five years. Simultaneously, English Puritans who failed to conform to the requirements of the Clarendon Code [1661–65] were harassed and scourged, though certainly with much less actual brutality than the Scots. The Huguenots of France were also soon to experience all the ferocity of a fanatical king and church. But the war that was now waged against Scottish Covenanters with a similar intensity pre-dated Huguenot troubles by almost a quarter of a century. If French Protestants suffered the rigour of the 'dragonades' in the 'eighties, the Covenanters met with similar woes, and even more tragic, in the 'sixties. Hunted mercilessly by the dragoons, some of them believed it right to meet force with force. Hence such encounters as those of Rullion Green [November 1666], Drumclog and Bothwell Bridge [both in June 1679], and Airds Moss [July 1680]. The murder of Archbishop Sharp of St. Andrews in 1679 further illustrates the state of desperation reached by a small section of the covenanting party. A larger number were willing to abide, not only in the kingdom, but also in the patience of Jesus Christ, and to wait prayerfully and courageously for the dawn of better days.

Many who could not be charged with the breach of any law were asked if they owned the King's authority. If they disowned it, they stood self-condemned; if they qualified their submission by distinguishing between Church and State, or if they declined to give their opinion, they were deemed equally guilty of treason. But, as Alexander Shields, the author of *A Hind let loose*, says: 'The more they (i.e. the authorities) insisted in this inquisition, the more did the number of witnesses multiply, with a growing increase of undauntedness, so that the then shed blood of the martyrs became the seed of the Church; and as, by hearing and seeing them so signally countenanced of the Lord, many were reclaimed from their courses of compliance, so others were daily more and more confirmed in the ways of the Lord, and so strengthened by His grace that they chose rather to endure all torture and embrace death in its most terrible aspect, than to give the tyrant and his complices any acknowledgment, yea not so much as to say, *God save the King*, which was offered as the price of their life'.

An outline of Scottish 'Covenant History'

Readers of the tragic story may thus be assured that the refusal of firm Covenanters to say 'God save the King' was not the result of any lack of true civil loyalty to 'the powers that be that are ordained of God', but solely the result of an enlightened conscience which refused to give to man, no matter how highly exalted in office he might be, the honour due to the Lord's Anointed. When such persons as the Solway martyrs ['the two Margarets'] refused to say 'God save the King', it was because of the meaning given to the expression by men in authority. Its use was tantamount to confessing that the King was supreme earthly ruler in the Church of God. The Covenanters chose death rather than life when impaled on the horns of the dreadful dilemma.

Shields' book, *A Hind Let Loose*, first printed in Holland in 1687, is a defence of the Covenanters. It expounds the belief that the King, though high in rank and office, is 'inferior to the people' whom he governs, and that their interests must take precedence over his. Ideally their interests are the same, but when the King shows himself a tyrant and a usurper of the rights of the Kirk, not to say of Christ the Head of the Kirk, ERGO [one of Shields' favourite words], he is to be resisted. Furthermore, if he is or becomes a Papist, how can he rule agreeably to the mind of God? The matter is argued with a vast abundance of Biblical illustration, and with much reference to Reformation and Puritan divines. It should be consulted, if practicable, by all who wish fully to understand the inner spirit of the Covenanting Movement.

In the ultimate issue the question at stake, in all its stark nakedness, was whether a temporal monarch or the Lord Jesus Christ was to be 'Head over all things to the Church'. To faithful Covenanters only one answer was possible, and whether their problems concerned individuals, families, conventicles, or general assemblies, they urged with fierce and unshakable tenacity that 'Jesus Christ is Lord'. No suffering could be too great to endure in such a cause. The scaffold could not daunt them; instruments of torture could not make them quail; the sufferings and discomforts of cave or moor or prison-cell could not move them to act and speak against conscience. Behind and above covenants subscribed with their hands and witnessed to by their hearts, and in an even truer sense subscribed in their blood, was 'the everlasting covenant, ordered in all things and sure', itself sealed with the blood of the Mediator, and itself the pattern of all lesser covenants. Faith gave buoyancy to the Covenanters' resolution; hope was the anchor of their souls; the love of Christ shed abroad in their hearts ever spurred them on to do and to suffer; 'outside the camp' they bore His reproach; and before them ever loomed large 'the recompense of the reward' and the gates of the city of God.

The 'Killing Time' eventually gave place to toleration and freedom. The overthrow of King James ii and the establishment of William and Mary on the throne brought liberty and enlargement. But whether faith and hope and love shone as brightly in Scottish hearts in the velvety days ahead as in the grim days which produced the Covenanting Movement, let those judge who can.

S. M. HOUGHTON

Bibliography

Anderson, James *The Ladies of the Covenant*, 1850

Barnett, T. Ratcliffe *The Story of the Covenant*, 1928
  The Makers of the Kirk, 1915
Barr, James *The Scottish Covenanters*, 1946

Carslaw, W. H. *Life and Letters of James Renwick*, 1893

Defoe, Daniel *Memoirs of the Church of Scotland*, 1717
Douglas, J. D. *Light in the North*, 1964

Fleming, David Hay *The Story of the Scottish Covenants*, 1904
Frazer, James *Memoirs of James Frazer of Brea*, 1847

Gilfillan, George *Martyrs, Heroes and Bards of the Scottish Covenant*, 1852
Guthrie, William *The Christian's Great Interest*

Hewison, J. King *The Covenanters*, 2 vols, 1908
Hodge, A. A. *The Confession of Faith*, 1870
Howie, J. *The Scots Worthies*, 1848
  Sermons in Times of Persecution in Scotland, 1880

Johnston, J. C. *The Treasury of the Scottish Covenant*, 1887

Kerr, James [Ed] *The Covenants and the Covenanters*, 1880
Knox, John *The Works of John Knox*, 1846

McCrie, Thomas *Vindication of the Covenanters*, 1845
MacFarlane, John *The Harp of the Scottish Covenant*, 1895

MacPherson, Hector *The Cameronian Philosopher: Alexander Shields*, 1932
The Covenanters under Persecution, 1956

Pollok, Robert *Tales of the Covenanters*, 1850

Renwick, James *Letters of James Renwick*, 1865

Rutherford, Samuel *Letters of Samuel Rutherford*, 1891

Shields, Alexander *A Hind Let Loose*, 1744

Simpson, Robert *Traditions of the Covenanters*

Smellie, Alexander *Men of the Covenant*, 1960

Stewart, James *Naphtali*, 1667

Thomson, J. H. [Ed] *A Cloud of Witnesses*
The Martyr Graves of Scotland, 1903

Walker, Patrick *Six Saints of the Covenants*, 2 vols, 1724–32

Wodrow, Robert *The History of the Sufferings of the Church of Scotland from the Restoration to the Revolution*, 2 vols, 1836

OTHER PAPERBACK TITLES

Not for sale to U.S.A. or Canada

OTHER TITLES

A Body of Divinity: Thomas Watson	328 pp.	15s.
The Christian Ministry: Charles Bridges	408 pp.	25s.
The Christian in Complete Armour:		
William Gurnall	1200 pp.	35s.
The Confession of Faith: A. A. Hodge	430 pp.	15s.
George Whitefield's Journals, illus.	596 pp.	25s.
*The Glorious Body of Christ:		
R. B. Kuiper	392 pp.	21s.
The Interpretation of Prophecy:		
Patrick Fairbairn	546 pp.	25s.
John G. Paton: Missionary to the		
New Hebrides	528 pp.	21s.
Lectures on Revivals:		
William B. Sprague	470 pp.	15s.
A Narrative of Surprising Conversions:		
Jonathan Edwards	256 pp.	15s.
The Office and Work of the Holy Spirit:		
James Buchanan	296 pp.	21s.
Robert Murray M'Cheyne: Memoir and		
Remains: Andrew A. Bonar	660 pp.	25s.
Simon Peter: Hugh Martin	160 pp.	12s. 6d.
Spurgeon: The Early Years, illus.	570 pp.	25s.
*Systematic Theology: Louis Berkhof	780 pp.	30s.
The Ten Commandments: Thomas Watson	240 pp.	15s.
*Thy Word is Truth: Edward J. Young	280 pp.	15s.

* *Not for sale to U.S.A. or Canada*

For free illustrated catalogue write to
THE BANNER OF TRUTH TRUST
78b Chiltern Street, London, W.1, England